Success in
your future.
Lily & Bill Foxon

Better Homes Cookery
THE QUICK COOK BOOK

Christine Watt

COLLINS LONDON AND GLASGOW

Contents

SECTION ONE *Quick Family Meals*

Quick cookery doesn't necessarily mean an endless succession of unadorned packet or canned foods, "fry-ups" and the inevitable canned fruit to follow! Quick cookery can mean attractive appetising meals for every occasion with the minimum of time and effort. I have tried to cut advance preparation and pre-cooking down to the minimum—although occasionally I do rely on

you, the reader, having cooked potatoes or rice as I think everyone has a surfeit of these by accident or intent from time to time.

The *Quick Cook Book* is in 2 main sections. The first contains recipes for family meals and the second includes rather more special recipes, suitable for serving to guests and friends.

When you are in a hurry try to dovetail food

The recipes in this section are for everyday family meals including soups, main courses and desserts. In the section on main courses I have given suggestions for the accompanying vegetables and sometimes the dessert course, to help you plan your meals more easily.

NOTE

Preparation time indicates approximate time it takes to prepare ingredients before the main cooking. *Cooking time* is the length of time the prepared dish takes to cook. Where no recipe is given for accompaniments these are suggested in *Serving suggestions*.

CHAPTER 1
Quick Soups

Although there are excellent canned and packet soups on the market, it is fun to use them occasionally, in combination with other ingredients, to produce a more substantial soup or a different flavour. I have also included some soups made from fresh ingredients which are very quick-to-make.

Brown Onion Soup

> *Preparation time: 5 minutes*
> *Cooking time: 25 minutes*
> *Special remarks: do not over-brown onions or they will spoil flavour of soup*
> *For 4-5 servings*

2 large Spanish onions
1-2 ounces butter
1 teaspoon sugar
2 pints good brown stock
salt and freshly ground black pepper

Melt butter and add the onions sliced in thin rings. Stir in sugar and cook for about 15 minutes until soft and golden brown. Heat the stock and pour it over the onions. Season to taste and simmer for 10 minutes.

preparation activities to make minutes count. Cook vegetables in the oven along with a main dish that is baked. Save on washing up by mixing ingredients for a recipe in one dish; use the baking dish or saucepan, if you can. Use paper bags for seasoned flour when coating meat or fish. Peel onions, apples, carrots or washed potatoes onto the paper in which they were wrapped—then it can be thrown away to keep your work top tidy.

You'll find lots of time-saving tips and ideas scattered throughout the book.

Quick Farmhouse Chowder

Preparation time: nil
Cooking time: 20 minutes
Special remarks: this soup makes an excellent and substantial snack meal
For 6 servings

1 (1-pint) packet thick farmhouse
vegetable soup
1½ pints water
1 (8-ounce) packet mixed frozen
vegetables
1 small can evaporated milk
salt and freshly ground black pepper

Combine contents of packet of soup and water. Bring to the boil, stirring occasionally, and add the frozen mixed vegetables. Reduce heat; cover and simmer about 15 minutes. Stir occasionally and add evaporated milk and seasoning just before serving. Serve with crisp, salted cracker biscuits.

Tuna Chowder

Preparation time: 5 minutes
Cooking time: 20 minutes
Special remarks: tomato or celery soup could be used instead of pea soup
For 4-6 servings

1 (1-pint) packet pea soup
1 small onion, finely grated
1½ pints water
1 small can tuna fish, roughly flaked
3-4 tablespoons rice, cooked
salt and pepper
chopped chives or parsley

Combine the pea soup, onion and water in a saucepan. Cook, stirring frequently until mixture boils. Cover and simmer for 15 minutes. Stir in the tuna fish and liquor. Add the rice and season to taste. Cook until heated through. Garnish with chopped chives or parsley.

Onion and Cheese Soup

Preparation time: 5 minutes
Cooking time: about 25 minutes altogether
Special remarks: this is a thick hearty soup
* —excellent for winter meals*
For 6 servings

2 ounces butter

3 large onions, very finely sliced
2 tablespoons flour
salt and pepper
2 pints milk
6 ounces Cheddar cheese, grated
toasted bread

Melt butter; add onions, cover and place over low heat. Stir. Then cook until soft—about 20 minutes. Stir in flour, salt and pepper. Add milk. Cook stirring constantly until mixture thickens and boils. Remove from heat; add cheese and stir to melt. Float toasted rounds of bread on top.

Instant Minestrone

Preparation time: nil
Cooking time: 20 minutes
Special remarks: mix everything in the saucepan and save washing-up!
For 4 servings

1 packet dehydrated mixed vegetables
2 stock cubes
1½ pints boiling water
1 tablespoon tomato purée
1-2 tablespoons pasta (macaroni,
vermicelli, alphabets, etc.)
salt and freshly ground black pepper

Put stock cubes in saucepan, add boiling water and dissolve. Mix in the dehydrated vegetables, purée, pasta and seasoning. Bring to boil, half cover and simmer for 20 minutes or until vegetables are cooked.

Brown onion soup, served with toasted rounds of bread sprinkled with cheese

Quick Garnishes for Soup

Quick farmhouse chowder is very easy to make. Garnish with crumbled crispy bacon or sprinkle paprika on top

Canned and packet soups are great time-savers. Add a simple attractive garnish and you have an appetising snack meal.

* Serve lentil or pea soup with finely sliced crisp-fried bacon.

* Toast slices of bread on one side only. Grate cheese onto untoasted side and toast until cheese is melted and bubbling. Cut in cubes and serve with onion or tomato soup.

* Add 2-3 tablespoons leftover cooked rice to tomato or clear vegetable soup.

* Garnish mushroom soup with whipped fresh cream.

* Cooked leftover sausages add body to vegetable or meat soups. Cut in thin rounds and heat in the soup for 10 minutes.

* Thin slices of lemon are delicious with clear soups especially tomato.

* Plain or herb-flavoured dumplings add bulk to meat or vegetable soups, turning a soup into a main course.

To make quick dumplings: mix 4 ounces self-raising flour with 2 ounces shredded suet, salt and pepper. Add sufficient cold water to make an elastic dough. Roll into tiny balls and add to the soup. Cover and simmer for about 15-20 minutes. To make herb-dumplings: add $\frac{1}{2}$ a small grated onion and $\frac{1}{2}$ teaspoon mixed dried herbs.

For lunch or supper serve Tuna chowder, made with canned and packet ingredients

CHAPTER 2

Quick Main Courses
Egg and Cheese Dishes

Omelettes are a boon to cooks-in-a-hurry. They are simple, quick to make and delicious to eat. If you imagine they're difficult to make follow the step-by-step photographs and simple rules and I guarantee success every time!

Have everything ready—filling, omelette pan, hot plate and accompanying vegetables before beginning to make an omelette. They must be served freshly made. Two or three eggs are used for each individual omelette and for this a pan with a 6 to 7-inch base is the most practical. An omelette pan should be thick and have rounded sides. It is preferable to keep the pan exclusively for omelette-making. If you do not possess an omelette pan use a small thick-based frying pan. It is important that the pan used is perfectly clean to start with. The butter should be sizzling hot (not brown) before pouring in the egg mixture. A common fault in omelette-making is not having the fat sufficiently hot before pouring in the egg mixture. Don't overcook the omelette or it will be tough.

Fluffy Cheese Omelette

Preparation time: 10 minutes
Cooking time: 5 minutes
Special remarks: fluffy omelettes are often sweet: add a teaspoon of sugar to the mixture instead of seasoning and fill with warm jam
Serving suggestions: hot rolls and butter
For 1 (2-egg) omelette

1 (½-pint) packet cheese sauce mix
½ pint milk
2 eggs, separated
good pinch salt
dash pepper
1 tablespoon warm water
knob of butter
radishes or tomatoes, to garnish

Make up cheese sauce with the milk according to packet directions. Keep warm.

Beat the egg yolks with the salt, pepper and water until creamy. Whisk the whites until they are stiff and stand up in peaks. Gently fold the whites into the yolks. Melt butter in omelette pan until sizzling and pour in the mixture. When the mixture has set on the bottom, place under a hot grill until omelette is puffed and golden on top. Serve at once with a little cheese sauce. Garnish with radishes or tomatoes.

Plain Omelette

Preparation time: 3 minutes
Cooking time: 3 minutes
Serving suggestions: green or tomato salad; sauté potatoes
For 1 (2-egg) omelette

2 eggs
1 tablespoon warm water
salt and pepper
knob of butter

Beat the eggs, water and seasoning lightly with a fork until well mixed. Add half the butter cut in tiny pieces. Heat the remaining butter in omelette pan until sizzling. Pour beaten eggs into hot fat and stir gently with back of fork. Push edges of omelette towards centre to allow uncooked mixture to flow underneath. When mixture is set and lightly brown underneath, tilt pan away from you and with a palette knife fold top and bottom thirds towards centre. Tip out onto a warmed plate. Serve at once.

Fluffy cheese omelette is served with creamy cheese sauce—a meal in a moment

TIME-SAVING TIP
For a really quick cheese sauce: chop 6 ounces soft processed cheese into small pieces. Put in a saucepan with 6 tablespoons milk. Heat very gently. Stir continuously until cheese melts and mixture blends into a smooth sauce. Use as required.

Stir rapidly with a zig-zag movement

Shake—keep omelette moving

Turn, handle up, and roll omelette out

Suggested Fillings

Quantities are for 1 (2-3 egg) omelette

FINES HERBES: Add 1 tablespoon fresh chopped herbs or 1 teaspoon mixed dried herbs to the omelette mixture.

POTATO: Dice some cooked potatoes and fry until brown in ½ ounce butter and ½ tablespoon oil. Add egg mixture and make omelette in usual way.

HAM: Add about 2 ounces chopped cooked ham and a teaspoon of fresh chopped parsley to the eggs before cooking.

SHRIMP: Drain canned or thaw frozen shrimps. Heat thoroughly in butter in a small saucepan with a few drops of lemon juice. Add to omelette before folding.

TOMATO: Peel and chop 2 tomatoes and cook in a little butter until soft. Add to the omelette just before folding.

MUSHROOM: Wash and slice 2 ounces mushrooms. Cook in butter, a little milk and seasoning until soft. Spoon into centre of omelette before folding.

FISH: Heat some cooked, flaked fish in a little cheese or creamy white sauce. Spoon into centre of omelette before folding.

PEASANT: Fry some slices of cooked potato in butter until crisp in a frying pan. Drain off excess fat and sprinkle with freshly chopped parsley. Add the egg mixture and make omelette in usual way.

KIDNEY: Wash and dry calves' or lambs' kidneys. Slice thinly and sauté in butter until cooked in a separate pan. Add a little brown stock or gravy and heat together. Make omelette in usual way and fill with kidney mixture just before folding.

SWEET CORN: Drain a small can of corn kernels. Cook over low heat in a small saucepan with a knob of butter, a little pepper and 3-4 tablespoons of thick cream. Fill each cooked omelette with a little of the mixture before folding.

Eggs à l'Indienne

Preparation time: 5 minutes
Cooking time: about 30 minutes altogether
Special remarks: you could use leftover cold cooked rice for this dish. Reheat with 1 ounce butter over low heat for 10 minutes
For 4 servings

8 ounces long grain rice
2 medium onions, finely chopped
2 ounces butter
1 level tablespoon curry powder
2 ounces raisins
juice of ½ large lemon
6 eggs
1 (½-pint) packet white sauce mix
½ pint milk
2 tablespoons parsley, chopped

Wash rice and boil until tender (about 15 minutes) in plenty of boiling salted water. Meanwhile cook onions in butter until golden brown and soft. Mix in the curry powder and cook, over low heat, for a few minutes. Pour rice into a strainer and rinse excess starch away with boiling water. Drain and stir into onion mixture with the raisins and all but 1 tablespoon lemon juice. Mix thoroughly and pile onto a hot serving dish. Keep hot. Hardboil the eggs then peel and quarter them. Arrange on the rice. Make the sauce according to packet directions adding the milk and remaining tablespoon of lemon juice. Coat the eggs with sauce and garnish with parsley.

TIME-SAVING TIP
Grate lots of cheese at one go! Wrap in grease-proof paper and a polythene bag. Use for sandwiches, toasted snacks and omelettes.

Macaroni Cheese Deluxe

Preparation time: 5 minutes
Cooking time: 30 minutes including boiling time for macaroni
Special remarks: choose pasta when you are in a hurry; it always cooks quickly

Serving suggestions: baked tomatoes
For 4 servings

6 ounces quick cooking macaroni
1 (5-ounce) carton cottage cheese
1 small carton fresh cream (thick or thin)
1 egg, slightly beaten
salt and pepper
4 ounces Cheddar cheese, grated
paprika pepper
parsley

Cook macaroni according to packet directions; drain well. Mix cottage cheese, cream, egg, salt and pepper. Add grated cheese and mix well. Stir in cooked macaroni and pour into a greased baking dish. Sprinkle with paprika pepper. Bake in a hot oven, 400°F or Gas Mark 6, for 20 minutes until brown and bubbling. Garnish with parsley sprig.

Quick Cheese Pudding

Preparation time: 5 minutes
Cooking time: 25-30 minutes
Special remarks: this dish can be made from the everyday contents of the store cupboard and is useful for unexpected guests

Serving suggestion: a green vegetable
For 4 servings

3 tomatoes, sliced
1 medium onion, sliced very thinly
6 ounces (4-6 slices) white bread
1 ounce butter
3 eggs
¾ pint milk
salt and pepper
pinch mustard
4-6 ounces cheese, grated

Grease a baking dish and cover with sliced tomatoes and onions. Season. Dice the bread and place in the dish. Dot with the butter. Beat the eggs and milk together; season well and add half the cheese. Pour over the bread pressing it down so that it absorbs the liquid. Sprinkle with remaining cheese and bake in a hot oven, 400°F or Gas Mark 6, until golden brown and puffy. Serve at once.

Macaroni cheese deluxe
—try this luxury way of serving a family favourite

Stuffed Pasta Rolls

Preparation time: 15 minutes
Cooking time: 25-30 minutes altogether
Special remarks: any type of hollow tubular pasta may be served in this way
Serving suggestions: French or Vienna loaf
For 4-6 servings

6-8 hollow pasta shells
FILLING:
6 ounces ricotta or cream cheese
2 ounces Parmesan cheese
1 egg, slightly beaten
2 tablespoons chopped fresh parsley
salt and freshly ground black pepper
3 ounces extra grated Parmesan or Cheddar cheese
SAUCE:
1 (15-ounce) can minced beef
1 medium onion, grated
1 clove garlic, minced or crushed
2 level tablespoons tomato paste
1 teaspoon dried basil
salt and freshly ground black pepper
1 teaspoon sugar

Cook the pasta in fast-boiling salted water for 15 minutes; drain in a colander and rinse with boiling water.

Mix the filling ingredients together—cheese, egg, parsley and seasoning. Fill the cooked pasta with the filling. Use a teaspoon or cut shells lengthwise with scissors and open to fill.

Mix the ingredients for the sauce together and put half the mixture in a flat shallow baking dish. Arrange the stuffed pasta in a row. Top with remaining sauce. Sprinkle with cheese. Bake in a moderate oven, 350°F or Gas Mark 4 until heated through and cheese is bubbling and brown.

Quick-Mix Pastry

8 ounces plain flour
½ level teaspoon salt
4 ounces whipped-up white fat
3 tablespoons cold water

Sieve flour and salt onto a piece of paper. Put 2 large tablespoons of this flour into a bowl. Add the fat and water. Beat with a fork for a minute. Add remaining flour and mix to a firm dough. Turn out onto a floured board and knead quickly and lightly until smooth. Roll out and chill if possible, before use.

Quick creaming (luxury) margarine may also be used for this pastry.

Egg and Tomato Pie

Preparation time: 15 minutes
Cooking time: 30 minutes
Special remarks: this pie reheats perfectly without spoiling. If you're going out, bake it and leave it for the family to heat up
Serving suggestions: green vegetable or salad
For 4 servings

8 ounces Quick-mix pastry
4 hardboiled eggs, sliced
2 tomatoes, peeled and sliced
4 rashers bacon, roughly chopped
salt and pepper

Use half the pastry to line an 8-inch flan or sandwich tin. Add the sliced eggs, tomatoes and bacon in layers. Season well. Cover with a lid of remaining pastry. Bake in a hot oven, 425°F or Gas Mark 7, until pastry is cooked and golden.

CHEESE AND ONION PIE: This can be made with 2 sliced onions mixed with 8 ounces grated cheese and a beaten egg.

Bacon and Egg Tart

Preparation time: 15 minutes
Cooking time: 30 minutes
Special remarks: this tart is delicious hot or cold
Serving suggestions: sauté potatoes; green salad
For 4 servings

6 ounces Quick-mix pastry
3 eggs
3 ounces cheese, grated
4-6 rashers lean bacon, rind removed
salt and pepper
about ½ pint milk

Use the pastry to line a 7-8-inch sandwich or flan tin. Prick lightly and line with paper and baking beans. Bake "blind" in a hot oven, 425°F or Gas Mark 6, for 5 minutes. Meanwhile chop the bacon and fry until crisp. Beat the eggs with the seasoning and milk; add bacon. Sprinkle base of pastry case with half the cheese and pour in egg mixture. Sprinkle with remaining cheese and bake in a hot oven, 400°F or Gas Mark 6, for 25-30 minutes until filling is set.

Photograph on left shows Stuffed pasta rolls

Rice and tuna pie

Haddock au Gratin

Preparation time: 10 minutes
Cooking time: 30 minutes
*Special remarks: any type of white fish
 may be used instead of haddock*
*Serving suggestions: baked or mashed
 potatoes*
For 4 servings

1-1½ pounds haddock fillet
½ ounce butter
salt and pepper
1 (½-pint) packet cheese sauce
½ pint milk
squeeze lemon juice
2 ounces cheese, grated
3 tomatoes, skinned

Cut fish in pieces, place in an ovenproof dish and dot with butter. Season with salt, pepper and lemon juice. Make up the sauce according to packet directions with the milk. Pour sauce over fish and sprinkle with cheese. Arrange sliced tomatoes around the dish and bake in a fairly hot oven, 375°F or Gas Mark 5, until cooked.

Oatmeal Fried Herrings

Preparation time: 5 minutes
Cooking time: 10 minutes
*Special remarks: herrings are excellent
 value for money—they are rich in
 protein and vitamins and always low-
 priced*

*Serving suggestions: boiled new potatoes;
 green beans*
For 4 servings

4 herrings, boned
milk
3 tablespoons oatmeal
2 ounces butter or oil
juice of 1 lemon

Dip herrings in milk and coat with oatmeal. Fry in hot butter until cooked. Pour lemon juice into pan and blend with the butter. Heat and pour over fish.

Rice and Tuna Pie

Preparation time: 10 minutes
Cooking time: 20-25 minutes
*Special remarks: you could use mashed
 potato instead of rice to make the pie
 shell*
Serving suggestions: any green vegetable
For 4-6 servings

2 cupfuls cooked rice
2 ounces butter or margarine, melted
1 small onion, grated
1 teaspoon mixed herbs (optional)
1 egg, beaten
1 (10-ounce) can condensed chicken
 soup
1 (medium) can tuna
1 (small) can pimiento (red pepper),
 chopped
1 tablespoon parsley, chopped

Mix the cooked rice, butter or margarine, onion, herbs, seasoning and egg together. Press into bottom and sides of a lightly buttered, shallow baking dish. Mix the soup, tuna fish (and liquor), parsley, seasoning and the pimiento together. Pour into the lined baking dish. Bake in a fairly hot oven, 375°F or Gas Mark 5, until slightly browned and heated through.

Sole and Broccoli

Preparation time: 15 minutes to make sauce and cook broccoli
Cooking time: 10 minutes to cook fish
Special remarks: you may prefer to glaze the finished dish under a hot grill before serving
Serving suggestions: sauté potatoes
For 4 servings

4-6 fillets of sole
1 large packet frozen broccoli
¼ pint milk
SAUCE:
1 ounce butter

1 ounce flour
½ pint fish liquor and milk, mixed
salt and pepper
1 egg yolk
juice of 1 lemon
1½ teaspoons sugar

Cook broccoli in boiling salted water according to packet directions until tender. Meanwhile season the fish fillets and place in a buttered saucepan. Pour ¼ pint milk around the fish and dot with butter. Poach over low heat for about 10 minutes or until cooked. Drain fish, reserving liquor, and arrange in a hot serving dish. Drain cooking liquor from broccoli and add a little butter and lemon juice to the broccoli to glaze it. Arrange around the fish; keep hot. To make sauce: melt butter in a saucepan and stir in the flour and seasoning. Gradually blend in the fish cooking liquor made up to ½ pint with milk. Bring sauce to the boil, stirring constantly, and cook for 2-3 minutes. Check seasoning and stir in remaining lemon juice, egg yolk and sugar. Pour over the fish fillets. Garnish with strips of peeled tomato.

Grilled Cod with Herb Butter

Preparation time: 10 minutes
Cooking time: 10-15 minutes
Special remarks: maître d'hôtel (herb)
butter is the classic accompaniment to
grilled or fried fish
Serving suggestions: mashed potatoes;
spinach
For 4 servings

4 cod steaks, fresh or frozen
seasoned flour
HERB BUTTER:
½ tablespoon fresh parsley, chopped
2 ounces butter
salt and white pepper
lemon juice
extra butter, for grilling
1 lemon

Wash fresh cod and dry with paper towels. Defrost frozen cod. Sprinkle with a little seasoned flour.

Herb butter: cream 2 ounces butter in a small bowl with a wooden spoon. Mix in the parsley, salt, pepper and lemon juice, to taste. If possible, chill before using. Remove grid from grill pan and heat the pan. Add a generous lump of butter and allow to melt. Place the prepared fish in the pan and divide Herb butter between 4 steaks. Grill under moderate heat basting frequently with the butter. The fish is cooked when the central bones can be removed easily. Serve the fish very hot with neat pats of Herb butter and lemon wedges.

Put washed fresh herbs in a jug and snip with scissors

Fish Mixed Grill

Preparation time: 5 minutes
Cooking time: about 20 minutes altogether
Special remarks: this attractive recipe
includes vegetables and everything is
cooked together
For 4 servings

about 1 pound white fish fillets, fresh or
frozen
2 ounces butter, melted
salt and pepper
4 tomatoes, halved
1 pound potatoes, cooked and sliced

Brush the grid of grill pan with melted butter and lay fish on it, skinned side uppermost. Arrange tomatoes and potatoes on grill, brush all the food with melted butter and season with salt and pepper. Grill under high heat for a few minutes then reduce heat to moderate. Turn the fish, brush with butter and continue grilling until cooked. To test: lift the flesh with the point of a knife; it should be opaque *not* transparent and a milky "curd" should form between the flakes of fish. Do not overcook fish or it will lose texture and flavour. The potatoes should be grilled for a few minutes longer to brown them thoroughly.

Baked Fish au Citron

Preparation time: 5 minutes
Cooking time: 20 minutes (see below)
Special remarks: any type of white fish
may be cooked in this way—allow a
cooking time of 10-20 minutes for
fillets, 20 minutes for steaks and 25-30
minutes for small whole fish
Serving suggestions: chipped or sauté
potatoes; brussels sprouts
For 4 servings

about 1½ pounds white fish
salt and pepper
2 tablespoons oil or melted butter
1 large lemon, thinly sliced
1 tablespoon fresh parsley, finely
chopped

Sprinkle fish with salt and pepper. Put the slices of lemon on the base of an ovenproof dish. Lay the fish on top, sprinkle with parsley and pour the oil or melted butter over. Cover with foil or buttered greaseproof paper. Bake in a moderate oven, 350°F or Gas Mark 5, until cooked.

Shrimp Curried Eggs

Preparation time: 15 minutes
Cooking time: 10-15 minutes
Special remarks: this makes an excellent
* supper dish*
Serving suggestion: boiled rice
For 4-6 servings

6 eggs, hardboiled
2 tablespoons mayonnaise
salt and pepper
1 teaspoon curry powder
good pinch dry mustard
1 (½-pint) packet white sauce mix
½ pint milk
1 (small) can shrimps
4 ounces breadcrumbs
1 ounce butter or margarine, melted
sprig parsley

Halve the hardboiled eggs; remove yolks and
mash. Mix with mayonnaise, seasoning and
curry powder. Re-fill egg whites; place in a
baking dish. Make up the sauce with the milk
according to packet directions. Add the canned
shrimps and a tablespoon of their liquor. Reheat
gently. Pour over the eggs. Mix breadcrumbs with
melted butter and sprinkle around edge of
mixture. Bake in a hot oven, 400°F or Gas Mark
6, for 10-15 minutes. Garnish with parsley.

Canned Salmon Pie

Preparation time: 10 minutes
Cooking time: 20 minutes altogether
Special remarks: use the cheapest canned
* salmon or tuna fish for this recipe*
Serving suggestions: diced carrots and
* peas*
For 4 servings

1½-2 pounds potatoes, peeled
1½ ounces butter
½ pint milk, plus 2-3 tablespoons
2 level tablespoons flour
1 (medium) can salmon
2 eggs, hardboiled
1 tablespoon fresh parsley, chopped
salt and pepper
2 teaspoons tomato concentrate
  (optional)

Boil and mash potatoes in usual way. Beat in a
walnut sized piece of butter and 2-3 tablespoons
milk. Melt remaining butter, stir in flour then the
milk and liquor from canned fish. Bring to the
boil and when sauce has thickened stir in flaked
fish, parsley, seasoning, tomato concentrate and
chopped hardboiled eggs. Heat mixture thoroughly
then pour into an ovenproof dish and cover with
creamed potatoes. Brush with melted butter or
milk and brown under a hot grill.

Haddock and Mushroom Bake

Preparation time: 5 minutes
Cooking time: 25 minutes
Special remarks: for a special occasion
  substitute fillets of sole
Serving suggestions: mashed potatoes;
  broad beans
For 4 servings

1 pound fresh or frozen haddock fillets
1 (1-pint) packet mushroom soup
scant ¾ pint milk
1 teaspoon Worcester sauce
4 ounces breadcrumbs
2 ounces butter or margarine, melted

Thaw frozen fish fillets. Place fillets in a greased shallow baking dish. Mix the soup with milk in a saucepan. Season with Worcester sauce, add a knob of butter and pour over the fish. Cover with foil and bake in a fairly hot oven, 400°F or Gas Mark 6, for 15 minutes. Mix butter with remaining ingredients; sprinkle over fish. Bake in a hot oven, 400°F or Gas Mark 6, for 10 minutes. Garnish with lemon and parsley.

Sole Piquant

Preparation time: 10 minutes
Cooking time: 5-10 minutes
Special remarks: whiting may also be
  prepared in this way
Serving suggestions: new potatoes;
  frozen peas or beans
For 4 servings

8 fillets of sole, washed
salt and pepper
lemon juice
3 tablespoons chutney
1 tomato, skinned
1 ounce sultanas or raisins
1 egg, beaten
6 ounces dried white breadcrumbs
deep fat for frying

Dry the fillets and sprinkle with salt, pepper and lemon juice. Mix the chutney, chopped tomato and sultanas or raisins together. Spread a little filling on each fillet. Roll up and dip first in egg then in breadcrumbs. Fry in hot deep fat until golden brown. Drain well and serve hot.

Fish Crumble

Preparation time: 10 minutes
Cooking time: 15-20 minutes
Special remarks: the fish may be cooked by poaching on top of the stove or baking in the oven
Serving suggestions: mashed potatoes; baked tomatoes
For 4 servings

1 (½-pint) packet savoury white sauce
½ pint milk
1 pound white fish, cooked
1 can garden peas, drained
salt and pepper
CRUMBLE:
2 ounces breadcrumbs
2 ounces flour
2 ounces butter
lemon wedges and parsley

Make up the white sauce with the milk as directed on the packet. Stir in the flaked, cooked fish and canned peas. Season well and pour into an oven-proof dish.

Make the crumble: mix breadcrumbs and flour, rub in butter. Sprinkle on top of the fish and bake in a hot oven, 425°F or Gas Mark 7, for 15 minutes. Garnish with lemon wedges and parsley.

Mackerel Baked in Foil

Preparation time: 5 minutes
Cooking time: 25-30 minutes
Special remarks: small fish are easy to prepare and have excellent flavour when cooked in foil
Serving suggestions: new or sauté potatoes; tomato or parsley sauce
For 4 servings

4 mackerel
salt and pepper
2 tomatoes, sliced
1 lemon, sliced
1 ounce butter

Clean the fish and remove heads. Season with salt and pepper. Place each fish on a good-sized piece of buttered kitchen foil. Arrange slices of lemon and tomato alternately on each fish. Top with a sprig of parsley and dot with butter. Fold the foil up and seal into neat parcels. Place on a baking sheet and bake in a moderate oven, 350°F or Gas Mark 4, until fish is thoroughly cooked. Serve in the foil.

Grilled halibut with Mushroom Sauce

Preparation time: 10 minutes
Cooking time: 15 minutes
Special remarks: try this easy way of making a sauce
Serving suggestions: mashed potatoes; green vegetable
For 4-5 servings

4-5 halibut steaks, washed
melted butter
salt and pepper
1½ ounces butter
2 level tablespoons flour
½ pint milk
3 ounces mushrooms, washed and chopped
few drops Worcester sauce
lemon wedges and parsley, to garnish

Wipe fish, trim and place on the grid of a greased grill pan. Brush with melted butter and sprinkle with salt and pepper. Grill under moderate heat, turning once. Brush occasionally with melted butter.

Meanwhile cook mushrooms until soft in about ½ ounce butter. Put remaining butter, flour and milk in a saucepan. Stir together and heat *slowly* until sauce boils and thickens. Add mushrooms and season with salt, pepper and Worcester sauce.

Serve fish garnished with lemon wedges and parsley.

Meat Dishes

In this section you will find meat dishes which are easy to prepare and cook. I have included a wide selection of dishes for you to choose from so that you can plan meals using different meats and different methods of cooking them. All the meat dishes in this section cook very quickly. You will find recipes in the Casserole section which are quick to prepare but take a longer time to cook.

It is important to choose the correct type and cut of meat for quick methods of cooking.

GRILLING OR FRYING

BEEF: rump; fillet or sirloin

VEAL: chops; cutlets or leg fillets

LAMB: chops (loin, chump or gigot); best end of neck cutlets; "fillets" from the top of the leg or shoulder

PORK: chops; cutlets; boneless slices from top of leg (fillet); thin slices of belly

BACON OR HAM: gammon slipper; middle gammon; corner gammon; back and ribs; streaky or prime collar

OFFAL: calves', sheep's or pigs' liver; kidneys; sweetbreads, brains

Many of the recipes are a combination of two methods of cooking, e.g. frying and braising or frying and roasting or frying and stewing or casseroling.

Lamb Chop Grill

Preparation time: 5 minutes
Cooking time: 15-20 minutes altogether
Special remarks: small pieces of fillet or rump steak may be substituted for the lamb chops
Serving suggestion: green salad
For 4 servings

4 thick lamb chops or cutlets
1 can tiny new potatoes or small cooked potatoes
melted butter
8 ounces sausages
salt and pepper
4 rashers bacon
4 tomatoes
3 ounces fresh breadcrumbs
2 ounces cheese, grated

Score fat edge of each chop. Fasten potatoes on skewers. Place chops and potatoes on the grill rack. Brush chops and potatoes with butter or oil and season. Grill for 10 minutes under moderate heat; turn. Add sausage and continue to grill for 10 minutes.

Meanwhile halve tomatoes and score cut surfaces, making ½-inch squares. Mix bread-crumbs and cheese and pile on each tomato half. Arrange on grill rack and cover chops with bacon rashers. Turn sausages. Brush potatoes again with butter and sprinkle with paprika pepper. Grill for a further 5 minutes.

Garnished Pork Chops

Preparation time: 10 minutes
Cooking time: about 25 minutes altogether
Special remarks: make sure pork chops are thoroughly cooked
Serving suggestions: mashed potatoes; braised or canned celery
For 4 servings

4 thick pork chops
1 ounce butter
1 onion, chopped
2 cooking apples, chopped
1 teaspoon ginger
1 tablespoon sugar
4 ounces breadcrumbs
salt

Cut away surplus fat from chops. Grill slowly on a medium heat for about 7 minutes on each side. Meanwhile fry the onion in hot butter until soft. Stir in the apples, ginger, sugar, breadcrumbs and salt. Cook gently stirring all the time for 5 minutes. Spread the stuffing mixture on each chop. Continue grilling for about 10 minutes or until stuffing is cooked and browned.

TIME-SAVING TIP

Coat fish, meat, chicken joints, etc., by putting seasoned flour in a strong paper or polythene bag and shaking to coat food—no mess all over the kitchen table and floor.

Steaks Bonaparte Trim fat from 4 ½-inch thick frying steaks. Brush with melted butter and season with steak seasoning. Fry quickly until cooked to your taste. Remove steaks and keep hot. Pour 1 tablespoon each lemon juice and Worcester sauce into frying pan, scrape to remove crusty sediment. Pour over steaks and serve, on fried bread if liked

Pork Chops and Savoury Rice

Preparation time: 15 minutes to cook rice
Cooking time: 20 minutes
Special remarks: use the same (breakfast-size cup to measure both the rice and stock
For 4 servings

2-3 rashers bacon, chopped
1 tablespoon oil
1 onion, chopped
1 green pepper, chopped
1 cup long grain rice
2½ cups stock
2 tablespoons canned tomato purée
salt and freshly ground black pepper
½ teaspoon mixed herbs
4 pork chops
seasoned flour
butter or lard, for frying

Wash rice. Fry the bacon until lightly browned in the hot oil. Add onion and pepper and fry for 5 minutes, until soft. Stir in the rice, stock mixed with tomato purée, herbs and seasoning. Bring to the boil, cover and cook over *low* heat for about 15 minutes or until rice is cooked.

Meanwhile coat the pork chops with seasoned flour and fry in hot fat until tender—15-20 minutes. Serve chops on a bed of rice.

Pork Chops in Chicken Sauce

Preparation time: 5 minutes
Cooking time: 30-40 minutes
Special remarks: choose your own favourite soup for this recipe
Serving suggestions: mashed or baked potatoes; peas or beans
For 4 servings

4 thick pork chops
seasoned flour
lard, for frying
1 (10-ounce) can condensed chicken soup

Trim the chops of excess fat and put this fat and the lard for frying in a flameproof casserole. Heat slowly to melt. Coat the chops with seasoned flour and brown quickly in hot fat. Pour off the excess fat and add chicken soup and ½ a soup can of water to the casserole. Cover and cook until chops are tender, stirring occasionally.

Devonshire Veal Cutlets

Preparation time: 5 minutes
Cooking time: 20-25 minutes
Special remarks: the sauce may be served separately, if you prefer
Serving suggestions: mashed potatoes; buttered carrots
For 4 servings

4 veal cutlets (neck)
1 tablespoon oil
1 ounce butter
lemon juice
salt and pepper
2 medium onions, chopped
1 cooking apple, grated
2 level tablespoons flour
¼ pint cider
¼ pint stock
fresh parsley, chopped

Beat the cutlets lightly. Sprinkle with salt, pepper and lemon juice. Heat butter and oil together and fry cutlets on each side until brown—about 10 minutes. Remove from pan and keep hot. Add extra oil if needed and fry onions until cooked. Stir in the apple and cook à few minutes more. Stir in the flour, then the cider and stock. Bring to the boil, stirring all the time until sauce thickens. Cook for 2-3 minutes more and season. Put the cutlets back into the pan and heat in the sauce. Sprinkle with parsley and serve hot.

Quick Curried Ham

Preparation time: 10 minutes
Cooking time: about 20 minutes altogether
Special remarks: try substituting a heaped tablespoon of chutney in place of the green pepper in the following recipe
For 6 servings

12 ounces rice
1 ounce butter
1 small onion, chopped
1 small green pepper, chopped
1 (10-ounce) can condensed celery soup
generous ¼ pint milk
12 ounces cooked ham, cut in chunky cubes
1 (small) can sliced mushrooms
1 dessertspoon curry powder
salt and pepper

Cook the rice in plenty of boiling, salted water for about 15 minutes or until just tender. Meanwhile fry the onion and green pepper in hot butter—cook until tender but not brown. Stir in soup, milk, ham, mushrooms (and liquor), curry powder and seasoning. Cook gently, stirring frequently, until heated through.

Tip rice into a strainer and pour boiling water through to rinse away excess starch. Melt a knob of butter in the saucepan—add rice and stir gently with a fork to mix. Cover and leave at side of stove (not over direct heat) until ready to serve. Pile curried ham on a bed of hot rice.

Corned Beef Casserole

Preparation time: 5 minutes
Cooking time: 40 minutes
Special remarks: everything—vegetables and all—is cooked in one dish in this recipe
For 4 servings

1 pound Brussels sprouts, washed
4 medium potatoes, boiled and sliced
¼ teaspoon thyme
salt and freshly ground black pepper
1 (12-ounce) can corned beef, cut in ¼-inch thick slices
about ½ pint stock (use a cube)

In a deep buttered casserole place a layer of potatoes then a layer of Brussels sprouts. Sprinkle with thyme, salt and pepper then add a layer of corned beef. Repeat with a final layer of ingredients ending with a layer of potatoes. Pour stock over all and brush potatoes with melted butter or oil. Cover and cook in a fairly hot oven, 375°F or Gas Mark 5, removing lid to brown potatoes for final 20 minutes.

Beef and Potato Pie

Preparation time: 10 minutes
Cooking time: 25 minutes
Special remarks: use leftover roast or boiled beef for this recipe
Serving suggestions: tomato salad or green vegetable
For 4 servings

1 ounce butter
1 ounce flour
generous ½ pint milk
salt and pepper
1 tablespoon freshly grated or 2 tablespoons prepared horseradish
about 12 ounces cooked beef, diced
1 (large) can new potatoes

Melt butter and blend in the flour. Gradually stir in the milk and cook until boiled and thickened. Season well. Add the horseradish. Mix the beef and potatoes and tip into a casserole. Pour the sauce over and bake in a fairly hot oven, 375°F or Gas Mark 5, until bubbling and golden brown on top.

Lamb Chops with Orange

Preparation time: 5 minutes
Cooking time: 15 minutes
Special remarks: serve 1-2 chops per person depending on appetite!
Serving suggestions: chipped or sauté potatoes
For 4 servings

lamb chops (loin, chump or neck)
oil or melted fat
salt and pepper
6-8 ounces mushrooms, sliced
2 oranges
1 bunch watercress, washed

Trim surplus fat from chops or cutlets. Brush with oil or melted fat and season with salt and pepper. Grill under moderate heat, turning frequently until tender—about 10-15 minutes altogether. Meanwhile fry mushrooms in oil or butter until cooked. Drain away excess fat and add juice of 1 orange, salt and pepper to pan. Heat, taking care to scrape away brown crusty sediment. Arrange cooked chops on a heated serving platter and add mushroom and orange mixture. Garnish with orange wedges and watercress.

Pigs-in-a-Poke

Preparation time: 5 minutes
Cooking time: about 35 minutes altogether
Serving suggestions: baked onions; mashed potatoes
For 4 servings

1 pound pork sausages
8 ounces bacon
2 large cooking apples
¼ pint stock or water and stock cube
salt and pepper
1 teaspoon dry mustard
1 tablespoon brown sugar

Brown sausages quickly under a hot grill or in a frying pan for 5 minutes. Remove rinds from bacon rashers and roll each sausage in a rasher of bacon. Core cooking apples and slice into rings. Poke a sausage and bacon roll into each apple ring and arrange in a shallow casserole. Mix stock, salt, pepper and mustard together and pour over sausages. Sprinkle sugar over top and cover with a lid. Bake in a hot oven, 400°F or Gas Mark 6, for about 30 minutes.

Quick Beef Goulash

Preparation time: 5 minutes
Cooking time: 30-35 minutes
Special remarks: alternatively use tender lamb, e.g. boneless slices of leg; or pork fillet
Serving suggestions: mashed potatoes; cabbage
For 4 servings

1 ounce butter
12-16 ounces rump steak
2 large onions, thickly sliced
1 clove garlic, crushed
1½ teaspoons paprika pepper
salt
1 teaspoon sugar
1 (medium) can peeled tomatoes
1 small carton soured cream

Heat the butter in a saucepan. Cut the meat in thin strips. Fry the meat and onions for about 10 minutes, stirring occasionally. Stir in the garlic, paprika, salt, sugar and tomatoes (with liquor). Cook for 10-15 minutes and just before serving remove from heat and stir in soured cream.

Beef Cobbler

Preparation time: 15 minutes
Cooking time: 20 minutes
Special remarks: this is a very useful recipe which can be made from the everyday contents of the store cupboard
For 4-6 servings

2 (16-ounce) cans minced beef and onions
1 (medium) can sliced green beans, drained
1 (10-ounce) can condensed tomato soup
1 packet scone mix
1 teaspoon celery seed (optional)
egg and milk (see packet directions)

Combine minced beef, green beans (with liquor), and soup in a casserole. Put into a hot oven, 425°F or Gas Mark 7, to heat while you prepare the scone mixture.

Tip scone mix into a mixing bowl; add celery seed and make up according to packet directions with egg and milk to mix. Cut scones into rounds and remove centres with a small round cutter. Brush with egg and milk and place on *hot* meat mixture. Return to oven and bake for about 15 minutes or until scone mixture is baked.

Peppers stuffed with Sausage

Preparation time: 15 minutes
Cooking time: 30-40 minutes
Special remarks: alternatively use minced meat instead of sausage meat
Serving suggestion: boiled rice
For 4 servings

½ ounce butter
2 medium onions, grated or minced
1 pound sausage meat
1 packet mushroom sauce
¼ pint milk
salt and freshly ground black pepper
1 tablespoon bottled brown sauce
3 tomatoes, skinned and chopped
4-6 medium-sized green peppers

Melt butter and sauté onions until beginning to brown. Stir in sausage meat and brown quickly over high heat. Drain off excess fat. Reduce heat and stir in sauce mix and ¼ pint milk. Bring to the boil and simmer 3 minutes. Season well and add brown sauce and tomatoes. Blanch peppers in boiling water for 5 minutes. Then remove stalks and discard seeds. Wash, dry and cut a thin slice from stem end so that they stand upright. Place in a baking dish containing 4 tablespoons water or stock. Fill each pepper with meat mixture and cover dish lightly with foil. Bake in a fairly hot oven, 375°F or Gas Mark 5, until cooked.

TIME-SAVING TIP
Use a coarse grater to make breadcrumbs for stuffings, puddings, etc.

Minced Meat makes Quick Tasty Main Courses

Hamburgers may be grilled under moderate heat—brush frequently with fat

Curried Mince Beef

Preparation time: 5 minutes
Cooking time: 40 minutes
Special remarks: alternatively minced lamb may be cooked in the curry sauce
Serving suggestions: plain, boiled rice; a selection of the usual accompaniments for curry, e.g. chapattis, poppadums, gherkins, sliced bananas, sliced tomatoes, pickled mango chutney, sliced onion, sliced hardboiled egg
For 4 servings

2 tablespoons oil
2 medium onions, chopped
1 cooking apple, peeled and chopped
1 tablespoon curry powder
1 teaspoon curry paste (optional)
1 tablespoon chutney or brown sauce
1 tablespoon flour
½ pint stock
2 ounces sultanas
1 tablespoon brown sugar
juice of ½ lemon
1 pound minced meat (beef or lamb)

Heat half oil in a large saucepan and fry onions and apple for 5 minutes. Stir in the curry powder, curry paste, chutney and flour. Then gradually mix in the stock. Bring to the boil and cook for 2-3 minutes. Stir in sultanas, sugar and lemon juice. Simmer sauce gently while you brown the meat quickly in remaining hot oil. Stir meat into sauce and continue to simmer for about 30 minutes.

Special Hamburgers

Preparation time: 10 minutes
Cooking time: 12-15 minutes
Special remarks: hamburgers should be handled carefully and cooked over moderate heat or they will be tough and dry
Serving suggestions: sauté potatoes; fried onions; green salad
For 4 servings

12 ounces raw beef
4 ounces bacon
1 small onion, peeled
1 teaspoon "made" mustard
1 teaspoon mixed herbs, fresh or dried
salt and freshly ground black pepper
1 small egg
dried breadcrumbs
oil or lard for frying

Mince the beef, bacon and onion together twice. Mix with the mustard, herbs and plenty of salt and pepper. Bind with beaten egg. Oil a sheet of greaseproof paper and roll the meat on this, into a thick sausage. Slice into ½-inch thick slices. Coat with dried breadcrumbs. Heat oil or fat in a frying pan. Fry hamburgers over moderate heat for 4-6 minutes, on each side, turning once. Garnish with fried onions.

When making lots of hamburgers use a small mould or measuring cup to shape them. Then flatten between squares of waxed paper

Quick chili con carne is full of flavour and can be served with boiled rice, potatoes or French bread

Savoury Beef Mince

Preparation time: 10 minutes
Cooking time: 50 minutes
Special remarks: you can add the washed, uncooked rice to the meat mixture with about ¾ pint stock and cook them all together for about 40 minutes
Serving suggestion: plain boiled rice
For 4 servings

1 ounce butter
2 onions, chopped
3-4 rashers bacon, chopped
1 small green pepper, chopped
2 ounces mushrooms, sliced
1 pound minced beef
1 (8-ounce) can tomatoes
½-1 teaspoon mixed herbs
salt and pepper
¼ pint stock
6-8 ounces rice

Melt butter and fry onion, bacon, pepper and mushrooms for 5 minutes. Stir in the meat with a wooden spoon to break it up. Fry for another 5 minutes, stirring all the time. Add the tomatoes (and their liquor), herbs, seasoning and the stock. Cover and cook stirring frequently for about 40 minutes or until all ingredients are cooked.

Meanwhile cook the rice as directed on page 25, Quick curried ham.

Quick Chili con Carne

Preparation time: 5 minutes
Cooking time: 40 minutes altogether
Special remarks: use good quality minced steak as it will cook more quickly
Serving suggestions: plain boiled rice
For 4 servings

2 tablespoons oil
2 onions, sliced
1 clove garlic, crushed
1 green pepper, chopped
1 pound lean steak, minced
1 (15-ounce) can tomatoes·
¼ pint water
2 teaspoons chili powder
½ teaspoon oregano
½ teaspoon paprika pepper
salt
pinch sugar
1 (large) can baked beans

Heat the oil and fry the onions, garlic, green pepper and steak together until well browned. Stir in the tomatoes and water. Bring to the boil and stir in the chili powder, oregano, paprika, salt and sugar. Simmer until tender, stirring occasionally. Just before serving add baked beans and reheat.

Meatball Pie

Preparation time: 10 minutes
Cooking time: 20-25 minutes
Special remarks: you can use a can of meat balls for this recipe instead of making them yourself
For 4 servings

MEAT BALLS:
  12 ounces minced steak
  4 ounces bacon, chopped
  ¼ teaspoon thyme or sage
  ¼ teaspoon paprika pepper
  ¼ teaspoon dry mustard
  salt and freshly ground black pepper
  1 small egg, beaten
  oil or lard for frying
SAUCE:
  1 large onion, chopped
  1 level tablespoon oil
  2 level tablespoons flour
  ¾ pint water
  1 beef stock cube
  2 teaspoons Worcester sauce
  1 (medium) can sliced carrots
  2 tablespoons parsley, chopped
TOPPING:
  1 French or Vienna bread roll
  butter
  2 tablespoons crisp rice cereal, crushed
  ½ teaspoon sesame seed

Meat balls: mix the meat, bacon, thyme or sage, paprika pepper, mustard, salt and pepper together and add beaten egg to bind. Form into small balls with floured hands. Fry meat balls in hot oil until cooked—about 15 minutes.

Sauce: meanwhile heat 1 tablespoon oil in a saucepan and fry the onion until soft. Stir in the flour then the water, stock cube and Worcester sauce. Season and bring to the boil. Cook stirring constantly until sauce thickens. Simmer for a few minutes before adding the carrots and parsley (add some of the carrot liquor if sauce is too thick). Drain the meat balls and add to the sauce. Mix everything together and pour into a greased ovenproof casserole.

Topping: cut French bread roll into slices; butter and arrange overlapping around the edge of the casserole. Sprinkle with crushed rice cereal mixed with sesame seed. Bake in a hot oven, 425°F or Gas Mark 7, for 10 minutes or until bread is crisp and brown.

Glazed ham steaks are baked in the oven with a delicious fruit glaze. Browned potatoes complete this easy main dish

Glazed Ham Steaks

Preparation time: 5 minutes
Cooking time: 45 minutes
Special remarks: you could grill the rashers if time is very short—they take about 15 minutes
Serving suggestions: spinach or brussels sprouts
For 4 servings

4 ham (or gammon) steaks, cut $\frac{1}{4}$ to $\frac{1}{2}$ inch thick
2 tablespoons oil
2 tablespoons brown sugar
4 tablespoons marmalade
pinch dry mustard
1 (small) can pineapple rings
little pineapple juice
cooked potatoes

Remove rind from rashers and snip the fat at 1-inch intervals. This helps to keep the rasher flat during cooking. Brush rashers with oil and arrange in a baking dish with pineapple rings in between. Mix brown sugar, marmalade, mustard and pineapple juice together. Spoon a little between each rasher. Arrange cooked potatoes in dish at same time and brush with oil. Sprinkle potatoes with salt. Cover and bake in a moderate oven, 350°F or Gas Mark 4, until ham or gammon is cooked. Remove lid for last 20 minutes to brown potatoes. Garnish with parsley.

Drain canned pineapple rings and cut in half. Arrange in a shallow baking dish alternately with the ham steaks

Spoon marmalade over steaks, or try honey or golden syrup, and sprinkle with ground cloves or ginger

Quick beef stew is made with handy store cupboard ingredients

Quick Beef Stew

Preparation time: 5 minutes
Cooking time: 25 minutes
Special remarks: you can prepare and
cook this stew in 30 minutes
Serving suggestions: crisp rolls or Vienna
loaf
For 4-5 servings

scant ¾ pint water
1 (1-pint) packet onion soup mix
3 medium potatoes, peeled and cubed
1 (8-ounce) packet mixed frozen
vegetables
2 (15½-ounce) cans stewed steak
little grated cheese

In a saucepan mix the water with the soup mix. When blended add frozen vegetables and potatoes. Bring to boiling point, stirring continuously. Cover and simmer for 15-20 minutes or until vegetables are cooked. Add the meat and heat thoroughly stirring occasionally. Season to taste. Pour into a hot serving dish and sprinkle a little cheese on top.

Kidneys and Rice

Preparation time: 5 minutes
Cooking time: 15-20 minutes altogether
Special remarks: cook kidneys over gentle
heat or they will become tough
Serving suggestions: plain boiled rice or
mashed potatoes
For 4 servings

2 ounces butter
1 onion, chopped
2½ level tablespoons cornflour
1 chicken stock cube
2 tablespoons red wine
¾ pint boiling water
8 lamb's kidneys, washed, skinned and
cored
salt and pepper
1 tablespoon tomato concentrate (paste)
4 ounces mushrooms, sliced

Heat half the butter and fry onion until cooked. Meanwhile fry the kidneys in remaining hot butter for 5 minutes. Mix the cornflour with the onion and blend in the stock cube dissolved in boiling water. Add the wine. Boil for 1 minute stirring all the time. Add the kidneys, seasoning, tomato paste and mushrooms. Simmer for 10-15 minutes or until kidneys are cooked.

Poultry

Nowadays, with the advent of frozen poultry and the young, always tender broiler chickens, it is possible to cook poultry quickly. Quick methods of cooking poultry, as with meat, are frying or grilling. A great variety of dishes can be made by combining methods of cooking, e.g. frying and braising.

FROZEN POULTRY: Must be defrosted slowly at room temperature; if you try to hurry up the slow defrosting process the flavour will be lost.

COOKED CHICKEN: This is widely available and may be used in salads or reheated by grilling or cooking in a sauce.

Devilled Chicken

Preparation time: 5 minutes
Cooking time: 50-55 minutes altogether
Special remarks: this is an excellent dish for a buffet party
Serving suggestions: new potatoes; green salad
For 4 servings

8 pieces of frying chicken
seasoned flour
½ teaspoon paprika pepper
oil for frying
1 (small) can devilled ham
½ tablespoon parsley, chopped
1 teaspoon prepared mustard
½ ounce fine dry breadcrumbs

Put the seasoned flour and paprika pepper in a strong paper bag. Add 2-3 chicken pieces and shake to coat them. Remove and continue with remaining chicken pieces.

Heat the oil and brown the chicken a few pieces at a time for about 15 minutes (leg pieces will take 20 minutes). Drain well on absorbent paper. When all pieces are browned put them back into the pan and continue cooking until chicken is done, turning from time to time.

Meanwhile mix the devilled ham, parsley and mustard. Spread over the cooked chicken pieces. Sprinkle with breadcrumbs and any brown crusty sediment from the frying pan. Cook under a hot grill until browned. Garnish with parsley and radish roses, if liked.

Speedy Orange Chicken

Preparation time: 5 minutes
Cooking time: 10-15 minutes
Special remarks: heating the spoon in boiling water before measuring syrup helps it to slide off easily
Serving suggestions: potato croquettes; garden peas
For 4 servings

2 level tablespoons cornflour
½ teaspoon ground ginger
2 level tablespoons golden syrup
1 can frozen orange juice and 2 cans water
4 large cooked chicken joints
1 orange, cut in thin slices (optional)

In a saucepan mix the cornflour and ginger. Stir in the golden syrup, water, and orange juice. Heat this sauce over moderate heat, for a few minutes.

Meanwhile heat the grill and put the chicken pieces on a baking sheet or plate which will fit on your grill rack. Brush the chicken with sauce and grill it under moderate heat until browned and heated right through. Keep basting chicken with sauce and turn pieces during cooking.

Add the orange slices, if used, for last 5 minutes of cooking time.

Chicken in Rich Tomato Sauce

Preparation time: 20 minutes
Cooking time: 40 minutes
Special remarks: the tomato sauce in this recipe is particularly good and can be served with other foods, e.g. steak; or add 8 ounces cooked ham instead of chicken and serve with spaghetti
Serving suggestions: buttered spaghetti, boiled rice, or potatoes
For 4 servings

1 frozen chicken cut into quarters or
    4 joints frying chicken
1 ounce butter
2 tablespoons oil
SAUCE:
½ ounce butter
1 tablespoon oil
2 medium onions, chopped
1 stick celery, chopped
1 carrot, grated
2 rashers bacon, chopped (optional)
1 clove garlic, crushed
1 (15-ounce) can peeled tomatoes
2 teaspoons sugar
1 teaspoon wine vinegar (optional)
scant ¼ pint stock or red wine
½ teaspoon salt
freshly ground black pepper
pinch oregano
pinch basil
fresh parsley

Defrost chicken (see frozen poultry page 34). Heat the butter and oil and fry chicken for about 20 minutes, turning once.

Meanwhile heat butter and oil for sauce. Add the onions, celery, carrot, bacon (if used) and garlic. Cover and sweat until vegetables are soft —about 10 minutes. Add remaining ingredients and bring to the boil, stirring continually. Allow sauce to bubble without covering the pan, for about 10 minutes.

Add chicken joints to sauce and cook slowly for a further 20 minutes.

Crisp Chicken Bake

Preparation time: 5 minutes
Cooking time: 20 minutes altogether
Special remarks: if time is very short heat all the ingredients (except crisps) thoroughly in the sauce. Pour into baking dish, top with crisps and brown under grill for a few minutes
Serving suggestions: tomato salad; sauté potatoes
For 4 servings

1 packet cheese sauce
½ pint milk
1 (medium) can celery hearts
12 ounces cooked chicken, cut in
    chunky pieces
salt and pepper
2 ounces Cheddar cheese, grated
2 packets potato crisps
parsley, to garnish

Using a large saucepan make up the cheese sauce with the milk according to packet directions. Drain the celery hearts and measure the liquid; make up to ¼ pint with extra cold milk. Stir into the sauce. Chop the celery and add, together with the chicken, seasoning and cheese, to the sauce. Mix everything together and pour into a baking dish. Cook in a hot oven, 400°F or Gas Mark 6, for 20 minutes; add the potato crisps 5 minutes before completion of cooking time. Garnish with parsley.

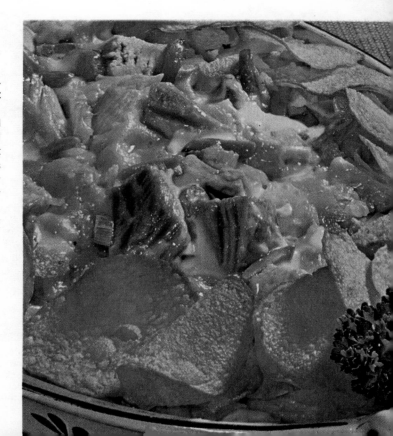

Chicken Fricassée

Preparation time: 5 minutes
Cooking time: 10-15 minutes altogether
Special remarks: evaporated milk makes a
good substitute for cream in many
recipes where a smooth texture is
required
For 4 servings

6-8 ounces long grain rice
8 rashers bacon, rind removed
1 packet mushroom sauce
½ pint milk
8 ounces cooked chicken and ham,
  chopped
5 tablespoons thin cream
1 egg yolk
fried bread

Cook the rice. Roll bacon, skewer and grill.
Make up the mushroom sauce as directed on the packet. Stir in the chicken and ham. Blend the cream and egg in a small bowl. Stir in a little hot sauce then stir into rest of sauce. Pour over a bed of cooked rice and garnish with bacon rolls and triangles of fried bread.

Chicken Maryland

Preparation time: 15 minutes
Cooking time: 5-10 minutes per chicken
joint
Special remarks: take care that the pan of
deep fat is no more than one-third full
Serving suggestions: creamy mashed or
sauté potatoes; peas or green beans
For 4-5 servings

1 (2½-3-pound) chicken, jointed
seasoned flour
1 egg, beaten
dried breadcrumbs
4 bananas
lemon juice
SWEET CORN FRITTERS:
1 packet batter mix
1 egg
¼ pint milk
1 small packet frozen corn kernels,
  thawed
butter for frying

Make up the batter as directed on packet using the egg and milk. The batter should be very thick. Add the corn kernels.

JOINTING A CHICKEN
The step-by-step photographs below show the easiest method of jointing a chicken. Chickens are jointed for most methods of cooking—follow the photographs and you can't go wrong!

1. Cut skin between thighs and body of chicken with a sharp 6-inch paring knife. Grasping one leg of chicken in each hand, lift until hips are free from the body

2. To remove the legs and thigh pieces, cut between hip joint and body close to bones at the back of chicken. Follow same procedure for other leg

3. If liked, separate thigh and leg. Locate knee joint by bending thigh and leg together. Cut through this joint to separate thigh and leg. Cut second leg

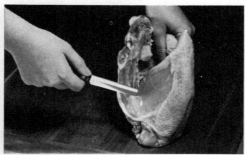

4. To remove the wings, pull wing away from body. Start cutting on inside of wing just over the joint. Cut down through joint. Remove other wing

5. Divide body by placing bird on neck end and cutting along the breast end of ribs to neck. Separate the breast and back section, cutting through the joints. Bend back piece in half to break at joint; cut through at this point with knife

6. To bone breast cut through white cartilage at V of neck. Grasp small bones on either side of breast. Bend each side of breast back; push up with fingers to snap out breastbone. If not boned, cut breast in two just below breastbone

Joint the chicken into fairly small portions. Dust with salt and pepper then coat with seasoned flour. Dip in beaten egg then coat with breadcrumbs. Press breadcrumbs flat with a palette knife. Heat the pan of deep fat and fry chicken joints a few at a time for 5-10 minutes. Drain chicken joints as they are cooked on absorbent paper and keep hot.

In a large frying pan heat about 2 ounces butter. Drop spoonfuls of the sweet corn fritter mixture in the hot butter. Fry until crisp and golden, turning them once. Fry the bananas for about 3 minutes in the hot butter, sprinkling them with lemon juice.

Serve the chicken with fried bananas and corn fritters. Bacon rolls may also be served.

Chicken Liver Risotto

Preparation time: 10 minutes
Cooking time: 25-30 minutes altogether
Special remarks: use the same cup to
*   measure the rice and stock*
For 4 servings

2 ounces butter
1 medium onion, finely chopped
1 pound chicken livers, chopped
4 rashers bacon
1 small red or green pepper
salt and freshly ground black pepper
1 level tablespoon tomato concentrate
**   (paste)**
2 cups rice
4 cups stock or water and stock cubes

Heat butter in a large heavy saucepan. Add onion and fry until pale golden brown. Add chicken livers and bacon and fry for 1 minute. Dip the red or green pepper in boiling water for a minute or two to soften. Then dry, remove seeds and chop finely. Add to the liver with the seasoning, tomato paste and rice. Cook stirring constantly for about 5 minutes. Stir in boiling stock and bring to the boil. Cover and cook over gentle heat until tender and all liquid absorbed—about 20-25 minutes. Stir the mixture from time to time with a fork to prevent sticking. It may be necessary to add a little more stock or water during the cooking. Serve hot, garnished with parsley.

Quick Chicken Curry

Preparation time: 10 minutes
Cooking time: about 45 minutes altogether
Special remarks: add more curry powder
*   if you like a "hotter" sauce*
Serving suggestions: plain boiled rice; a
*   selection of curry accompaniments, e.g.*
*   chutney, raisins, coconut or chopped*
*   cucumber and peanuts*
For 4-5 servings

1 cooked chicken or 4 large cooked
**   chicken joints**
SAUCE:
2 tablespoons oil
2 onions, sliced
1 cooking apple, chopped
2-4 ounces mushrooms, washed and
**   sliced**
1 tablespoon curry powder
1 level teaspoon flour
½ pint stock
½ tablespoon brown sauce
squeeze lemon juice
1 tablespoon chutney
½ level teaspoon salt
1 ounce sultanas

Heat the oil and add the onions; cover and cook for 5 minutes over low heat. Add apple and mushrooms; fry for a few minutes more. Stir in the curry powder and flour. Gradually stir in the stock, brown sauce, lemon juice, chutney, salt, and sultanas. Cook for a few minutes.

Meanwhile remove flesh from chicken and chop roughly; add to sauce. Cover and reduce heat. Simmer for 20-30 minutes until sauce has thickened. Garnish with parsley.

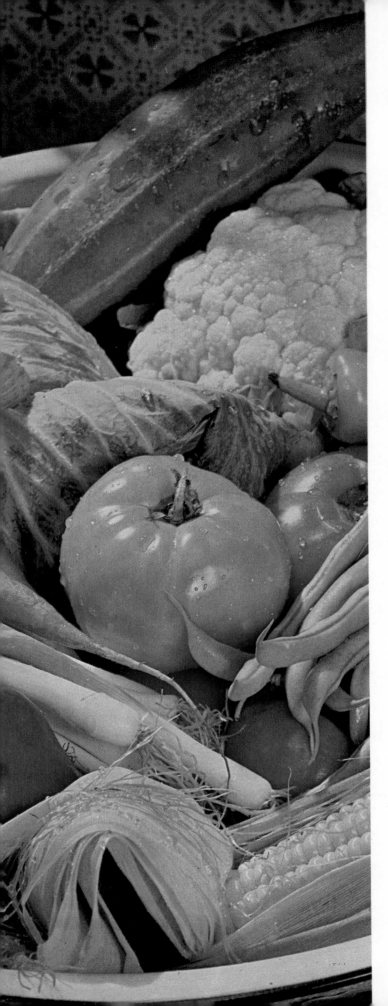

CHAPTER 3

Vegetables and Salads

In this section you will find recipes to make the most of vegetables whether fresh, frozen, canned or dried. Vegetable cookery is often the most neglected and badly carried out part of the meal. Don't be afraid to try the lesser known types of vegetables, to add interest and flavour to meals. A general rule of vegetable cookery is to cook fresh vegetables in the *minimum* amount of *boiling, salted* water and cook as rapidly as possible with the lid on the pan. In this way you retain the maximum amount of valuable vitamins and mineral salts.

The most time-consuming part of vegetable cookery is the preparation. Save time and bother by buying twice the quantity you need for one meal. Prepare vegetables then wash, shake dry and store in polythene bags in the refrigerator.

Potatoes can be cooked in advance—the best way is to scrub but not peel them. Put in boiling salted water and cook gently until tender. The cooked potatoes can be stored and, when they are required, peeled and fried for sauté potatoes, made into croquettes, or used in any of the recipes using cooked potatoes.

I have only dealt in this section with vegetables which are fairly quick and simple to prepare and cook.

Fried Aubergines

Preparation time: 2-3 minutes
Cooking time: 6-8 minutes
Special remarks: aubergines are long oval-shaped vegetables with a shiny purple skin
For 4 servings

2-3 aubergines
seasoned flour
butter or oil, for frying

Cut off the stem and small leaves from the aubergines. Then wash and if skin is blemished, peel. Slice about ½ inch thick, removing coarse seeds. Then fry in hot butter or oil until cooked.

Broad Beans

Choose young beans with well-filled pods. Shell and cook in boiling salted water until soft.

Canned broad beans have a good flavour. Make up a packet of savoury parsley sauce using the liquid from the can plus extra milk to make the required quantity. When boiling add the beans and heat gently. Add extra chopped fresh parsley.

French and Runner Beans

Top, tail and string the beans then slice thinly or cut across in 1-inch lengths. Boil 1 inch water in a saucepan. Add 1 teaspoon salt and the beans. Cover and boil rapidly until just tender. Drain and toss with a knob of butter.

Dutch Green Beans

Preparation time: 5 minutes
Cooking time: 10 minutes
Special remarks: French or runner beans
  are also called green beans
For 4 servings
1 small onion, sliced
1 ounce butter
1 (8-ounce) packet frozen green beans
4 tablespoons water
½ teaspoon salt

Cook onion in butter until soft but not brown. Add water and bring to the boil. Add beans and salt, bring to boiling point. Cover, reduce heat and simmer until cooked.

For canned beans, add the beans and liquor but no water to the onion and heat through.

Broccoli

There are several varieties of this vegetable but the most common is the sprouting broccoli which has green or purple heads like cauliflower heads on a stalk. Cook like any other green vegetable allowing 15-20 minutes. Serve with butter. Frozen broccoli has a very good flavour—cook as directed on packet and add seasoning, lemon juice, butter and a teaspoon of sugar.

Brussels Sprouts

These are available fresh, frozen or dehydrated. Wash sprouts, removing discoloured outside leaves, and cut a cross in the base of large ones.

Cook rapidly in boiling, salted water until just tender—10-15 minutes. Drain and toss with butter.

Crunchy Brussels sprouts can be made by boiling fresh or frozen sprouts until tender. Then drain, add butter and serve sprinkled with toasted crumbs and grated Parmesan cheese.

Cabbage

Green cabbage (Savoy or Dutch) should be cut in half and the coarse outer leaves and hard centre stalk removed. Wash. Shred finely and cook in 1-2 inches boiling water with ½ teaspoon salt, 1 teaspoon sugar and a pinch of dry mustard added. Boil rapidly until cooked—10-15 minutes. Drain well and add a knob of butter and a sprinkling of pepper. Serve at once.

Spring greens (Spring cabbage) should be cooked in the same way but does not take quite so long to cook.

Red cabbage is sold fresh and can be pickled or canned—it makes an excellent accompaniment to cold meats.

Fried Cabbage

Preparation time: 5 minutes
Cooking time: 15 minutes
For 4 servings
3 rashers bacon, rind removed
½ head Dutch cabbage
1 tablespoon lemon juice
salt and pepper

Fry bacon until brown and crisp in a little hot butter; remove from pan. Wash and shred cabbage finely. Cook in hot fat until tender adding extra butter if required. Season with lemon juice, salt and pepper. Serve garnished with bacon.

Carrots

New carrots can be scraped, washed and cooked whole. Simmer in salted water for about 15 minutes. Old carrots should be peeled and cut in thin rounds or strips and cooked for 20 minutes. Serve tossed with butter, pepper and chopped fresh parsley.

Glazed Carrots

Preparation time: 5 minutes
Cooking time: 20-25 minutes
For 4 servings

Drain a can of green beans. In a saucepan melt 1 ounce butter or margarine, ½ teaspoon dry mustard, salt and pepper. Add beans, cover and heat gently. Serve sprinkled with Parmesan cheese

1 pound young carrots, scraped
1 ounce butter or margarine
½ level teaspoon salt
pinch pepper
pinch dry mustard
2 teaspoons sugar
stock or water
chopped parsley

Melt butter. Add carrots, salt, pepper, mustard and sugar. Add enough stock or water to come half-way up the carrots. Bring to the boil, reduce heat and cook without a lid until tender and liquid has almost all evaporated. Serve sprinkled with parsley.

Frozen or canned beans are delicious served with glazed button onions

Cauliflower

Break cauliflower into sprigs, discarding coarse stems. Wash and cook with the stems on the base of the pan in boiling salted water for 10-15 minutes. Drain and serve with butter or plain or cheese sauce.

Chicory

This vegetable is very easy to prepare—simply wash the thick white heads. Plunge into boiling salted water, adding a squeeze of lemon juice. Reduce heat and cook for 20 minutes. Drain and add melted butter and a pinch of sugar. Or serve with cheese or tomato sauce.

Corn Kernels and Onions

Preparation time: 5 minutes
Cooking time: 10 minutes
For 4 servings

2 ounces butter or margarine
1 small onion, sliced
2 tomatoes, peeled and chopped
salt
1 (medium) can corn kernels or 1 packet frozen corn kernels

If using frozen corn, cook as directed on packet. Meanwhile melt butter in a saucepan, add onion, cover and cook over low heat for 4-5 minutes, stirring occasionally. Add roughly chopped tomato and corn kernels. Mix and heat thoroughly. Season to taste.

Leeks au Gratin

Preparation time: 10 minutes
Cooking time: 30 minutes
For 4 servings

4-8 leeks, depending on size
½ pint savoury white sauce
1 ounce butter, melted

Remove coarse outside leaves and cut off tops about 2 inches above the white part. Cut off roots and split lengthwise almost to the base—wash very thoroughly under running water, making sure all grit and soil has been removed. Cook in boiling salted water until soft. Meanwhile prepare savoury white sauce. Drain leeks well and arrange in a shallow buttered baking dish. Coat with sauce and pour melted butter over. Brown under a medium grill.

Mushrooms

Cultivated mushrooms do not have to be peeled. Simply wash and drain, then trim away the earthy end of the stalk.

TO BAKE: place in a greased baking dish with pats of butter. Season and cover with a lid or foil. Bake until tender—about 20 minutes.

TO POACH: simmer in a saucepan with a little milk and salt and pepper until tender.

TO GRILL: brush with oil or melted butter and grill for about 4 minutes, turning once.

TO FRY: fry in hot butter, oil or bacon fat until cooked.

Grate sharp Cheddar cheese straight onto hot vegetable

Onions

These are now available in dried form as de-hydrated flakes and as onion salt.

Glazed Onions

> *Preparation time: 5 minutes*
> *Cooking time: 15 minutes*
> *Special remarks: button onions may be prepared in this way but as they are time consuming to peel allow a longer preparation time*
> *For 4 servings*
>
> **4 medium onions, skinned**
> **2 ounces butter**
> **2 teaspoons sugar**

Slice the onions and cook until tender in enough boiling salted water to just cover, without a lid. Boil rapidly to evaporate any remaining liquid. Add the butter and sugar. Shake in the pan over gentle heat until glazed.

Baked Onions

> *Preparation time: 5 minutes*
> *Cooking time: 45-60 minutes*
> *For 4 servings*
>
> **4 medium onions**
> **pieces of foil**
> **melted butter, to serve**

Wash onions but do not peel. Wrap in foil and stand in a baking tin. Cook in a moderate oven, until soft when squeezed. Serve in the foil with melted butter.

Peas

Peas can be bought ready shelled, or alternatively you can use frozen, dehydrated or canned peas. To retain flavour of frozen peas cook in $\frac{1}{2}$ inch boiling salted water with a teaspoon of sugar and fresh or dried mint added. Drain and toss with a knob of butter.

Canned garden peas can be drained of their liquid then heated gently with a knob of butter, salt, pepper and a pinch of sugar. If you have a few lettuce leaves shred them finely and add to frozen peas before cooking—they add a lovely flavour. A little grated onion also adds to the flavour of canned or frozen peas.

Potatoes

Potatoes should be peeled as thinly as possible— new potatoes are scraped or brushed. The quickest

A pinch of dried basil adds a subtle flavouring to carrots. Add to the cooking water, drain and glaze with butter

way of preparing potatoes is to scrub them well and cook in their skins.

Boiled Potatoes

Preparation time: 10 minutes
Cooking time: 15-20 minutes for new potatoes, 20-30 minutes for old
Special remarks: old potatoes should be put in cold water, new potatoes may be put into boiling water
For 4 servings

2 pounds potatoes
1-2 ounces butter
chopped chives, spring onions or parsley, to serve

Peel potatoes thinly and cut into uniformly sized pieces. Put in a saucepan with enough cold salted water to cover. Put on the lid and boil gently until tender. Drain, dry off over low heat and serve with butter and chopped herbs.

CREAMY MASHED POTATOES: boil as above then drain and dry off with butter and 2 tablespoons milk or thin cream. Mash well over heat and season with salt, pepper and a pinch of ground nutmeg. The electric mixer may be used for extra smooth potatoes.

DUCHESSE POTATOES: cook as for boiled potatoes and after drying off, sieve potatoes to remove all lumps. Add a little butter, milk, seasoning and 1 egg to every pound of potatoes. Beat well. Using a large forcing bag with a large nozzle, pipe in pyramids onto a greased baking sheet. Brush carefully with melted butter or beaten egg. Bake until brown in a hot oven, 425°F or Gas Mark 7.

CROQUETTES: you can make these with leftover boiled or mashed potatoes. Sieve and add seasoning and 1 egg for every pound of potatoes. Beat well. Form into rounds, rolls or

Devilled beef salad

balls with floured hands. Brush with beaten egg and coat with browned breadcrumbs. Fry in deep fat until golden brown. Alternatively fry in a little shallow fat.

CHIPPED POTATOES: peel potatoes and cut into chips. Rinse well to remove surface starch. Drain and dry thoroughly in a clean cloth. Fill a deep pan of frying oil or fat not more than one-third full and heat. Place chips in frying basket and lower gently into fat. Fry until golden brown—7-10 minutes. Drain well and serve at once sprinkled with salt.

BAKED JACKET POTATOES: choose potatoes of even size, scrub well and dry. Brush skins with oil to make them taste better. Put on oven shelf and bake until they feel soft when squeezed in a cloth. Prick to allow steam to escape, then cut a cross on top. Squeeze gently in a cloth to make the points open. Season and serve with a knob of butter.

SAUTE POTATOES: use parboiled or completely cooked potatoes. Slice thickly and fry in butter or oil until crisp and brown on both sides.

Scalloped Potatoes

Preparation time: 10 minutes
Cooking time: 40-60 minutes
For 4 servings

1 pound potatoes, in $\frac{1}{8}$-inch thick slices
1 large onion, chopped
1 ounce butter
$\frac{1}{4}$-$\frac{1}{2}$ pint milk
salt and freshly ground black pepper
1 (5-ounce) carton plain yoghurt or thin cream
1 rounded teaspoon flour

Put layers of potatoes and onion in a baking dish. Season well with salt and pepper. Boil milk with butter and pour over potatoes. Mix yoghurt or cream with flour and pour over potatoes. Put in a hot oven, 400°F or Gas Mark 6, and bake until potatoes are cooked.

Spinach

Fresh spinach should be washed in several changes of water. Cook in a saucepan with only the water which clings to the leaves. Heat gently, turning spinach over, then heat to boiling. Reduce heat and cook gently until soft—10-15 minutes. Drain and serve with butter and seasoning.

CREAMED SPINACH: sieve cooked spinach (or use cooked frozen or canned spinach) and

Mexican salad

add 2 tablespoons cream and some seasoning. Re-heat gently.

Tomatoes

GRILLED: cut in half and place on grill rack, cut side uppermost. Brush with melted fat and season. Grill 5-10 minutes.

BAKED: cut tomatoes in half or if required whole cut a cross lightly on top. Brush with fat, season, cover and bake for 15 minutes.

Turnips

Peel thickly and cut in small slices or dice. Cook in boiling, salted water, with a teaspoon of sugar added, for 20 minutes. Serve well-drained, with a knob of butter and chopped fresh parsley.

Devilled Beef Salad

Preparation time: 5 minutes
Cooking time: nil
Special remarks: this is a main-dish salad
For 4 servings

1 large lettuce, washed
8-12 ounces roast beef, cut in strips
8 ounces small tomatoes
1 onion, thinly sliced in rings
1 (small) can anchovy fillets, drained and rinsed
MUSTARDY HORSERADISH DRESSING:
$\frac{1}{4}$ level teaspoon salt
$\frac{1}{8}$ level teaspoon pepper
1 teaspoon dry mustard
1 teaspoon sugar
1 tablespoon freshly grated or prepared horseradish
2 tablespoons vinegar
4 tablespoons oil

In a salad bowl toss the lettuce, onion rings and anchovies. Arrange tomatoes and beef on the salad.

Dressing: put all ingredients in a screw-topped bottle—shake vigorously and pour over the salad.

Salads

Salads make excellent main courses as well as accompaniments to meat and poultry dishes. They are quick to prepare, full of flavour and packed with vitamins.

Mexican Salad

Preparation time: 5 minutes
Cooking time: 40 minutes
Special remarks: this is a main-dish salad
Serving suggestion: crisp rolls
For 4 servings

1 pound minced steak
half (1-pint) packet onion soup mix
scant $\frac{1}{2}$ pint water
salt and freshly ground black pepper
dash tabasco sauce (optional)
1 medium head lettuce, washed
2 tomatoes, cut in wedges
1 small onion, thinly sliced in rings
2 ounces grated cheese
a few black olives, sliced
1 small packet potato crisps or corn crisps

Brown meat without fat in a frying pan. Sprinkle the onion soup over meat and stir in water. Simmer uncovered for 30 minutes, stirring frequently.

Pull the lettuce into pieces and toss in a salad bowl with onion, green pepper, cheese and olives. Pile meat in centre and garnish with tomato wedges and crushed crisps.

Rice Salad

Preparation time: 10 minutes
Cooking time: 20 minutes
Special remarks: rice is becoming a popular "vegetable" instead of potatoes
For 3-4 servings

1 cup rice
2 cups chicken stock
1 large onion, sliced
4 rashers lean bacon, chopped
2 ounces mushrooms, chopped
1 small packet frozen peas, cooked
1 hardboiled egg

Wash rice thoroughly. Put in a saucepan with the chicken stock and $\frac{1}{2}$ teaspoon salt. Bring to the boil, cover with a close-fitting lid and simmer for 14-17 minutes without stirring. Remove the lid and test rice—if not cooked replace lid and cook another few minutes. Fluff rice with a fork.

Meanwhile fry onion and bacon together in a little butter. Mix in the mushrooms and continue to fry a few minutes more. Drain and using a fork mix into the rice together with the peas. Pile in a dish and serve hot or cold garnished with hardboiled egg.

Rice salad is served as an alternative to potatoes with meat dishes. It can be served hot or cold.

Piquant Sauce for Vegetables

Preparation time: 5 minutes
Cooking time: 5 minutes
Special remarks: particularly good with broccoli, asparagus, cauliflower or baked potatoes
For 4 servings

1 (½-pint) packet cheese sauce
scant ½ pint milk
1 small carton plain yoghurt
2 teaspoons chopped chives, parsley or dried dill

Make up the cheese sauce according to packet directions using less milk than usual. When cooked add the yoghurt and herbs, heat through and pour over the cooked vegetable.

Creamy Green Beans

Preparation time: 2 minutes
Cooking time: 10-15 minutes
Special remarks: you could serve cooked fresh beans in the same way
For 4 servings

1 (8-ounce) packet frozen green beans
4 tablespoons thick cream
½ teaspoon celery salt
pinch sugar

Cook beans according to packet directions but do not salt the water. Meanwhile beat cream with salt and sugar lightly. Drain beans and tip into heated serving dish. Spoon sauce over.

Herbed tomato slices Cut 3 large tomatoes in half. Arrange in a baking dish. Sprinkle with salt. Mix 3 ounces fresh breadcrumbs with 2 ounces melted butter or margarine and ¼ teaspoon dried basil. Sprinkle on tomatoes. Bake uncovered in a moderate oven, 350°F or Gas Mark 4, for 20-25 minutes. Makes 6 servings.

Tomato Salad

Preparation time: 2 minutes
Cooking time: nil
Special remarks: an excellent accompaniment to all meat dishes
For 4 servings

6 large ripe tomatoes
2 tablespoons oil
salt
freshly ground black pepper
a few green onion tops
sprig parsley

Plunge tomatoes in boiling water for a minute and remove skins. Slice and arrange in one layer in a flat dish. Season with oil, salt and pepper. Sprinkle liberally with chopped onion tops and parsley.

Coleslaw Salad

Preparation time: 10 minutes
Cooking time: nil
Special remarks: this salad can be prepared in advance and kept (covered) in the refrigerator for 2 or 3 days
For 4 servings

4 tablespoons coleslaw dressing (or salad cream)
¼ teaspoon dry mustard
squeeze lemon juice
salt and freshly ground black pepper
½ medium hard white cabbage, washed and finely shredded
1 carrot, grated
1 small onion, grated
1 tablespoon chopped parsley
1 stick celery, chopped (optional)

Put the dressing or salad cream, mustard, lemon juice and seasoning in a salad bowl. Blend together. Add prepared remaining ingredients and mix thoroughly.

Hot and Cold Desserts

You will find lots of ideas in this section for hot puddings and cold sweets. I have specially chosen simple recipes which require little preparation and cooking. It is amazing how many delicious desserts can be made from a few simple ingredients—have a look at the French fritter, fruit and ice cream sauce recipes. The majority of dessert recipes can be prepared and made in less than 30 minutes.

Apricot Coconut Pudding

Preparation time: 10 minutes
Cooking time: 25-30 minutes
Special remarks: mandarin oranges or pineapple may be used instead of apricots
For 4-6 servings

1 (medium) can apricot halves
1 ounce butter or margarine
2 level tablespoons brown sugar
3-4 level tablespoons desiccated coconut
1 (6½-ounce) packet sponge mix
1 egg
GLAZE:
2 level tablespoons cornflour
2 level tablespoons brown sugar
rind and juice of 1 orange

Drain apricots, reserving juice. Mix butter or margarine, brown sugar and 3 tablespoons apricot juice in a small saucepan. Stir until butter melts then mix in the coconut and pour into a greased cake tin. Arrange apricots in centre.

Prepare packet sponge mix as directed and pour over apricots. Bake in a hot oven, 400°F or Gas Mark 6, until sponge is cooked.

Meanwhile prepare glaze: mix cornflour and brown sugar. Stir in the remaining apricot juice and orange rind. Bring to boil, cook until mixture is thickened. Add enough orange juice to thin mixture to a coating consistency.

Allow sponge to cool in the tin for a minute before inverting onto a serving plate. Spoon glaze over top and sides. Serve warm or cold.

Fruit Fool

Preparation time: 10 minutes
Cooking time: nil
Special remarks: drain the fruit really well for this sweet—the juice can be used for a jelly or fruit sauce
For 4 servings

1 can soft fruit (gooseberries, strawberries, apricots, etc.)
1 (4-5-ounce) carton thick cream
2 teaspoons lemon juice
sponge fingers or biscuits, to serve

Drain fruit and push through a sieve or purée in the electric liquidiser. Add lemon juice. Whisk cream until very thick. Fold the fruit gradually into the cream using a tablespoon. Pour into glasses and chill before serving.

Quick Trifle

Preparation time: 10 minutes
Cooking time: nil
Special remarks: you could use thick egg custard sauce instead of fresh cream
For 4 servings

1 small jam swiss roll or piece of leftover sponge cake
2 tablespoons sherry
jam—preferably apricot
1 (medium) can peaches
1 (4-5-ounce) carton thick cream
4 tablespoons thin cream or top-of-the-milk
1 large chocolate flake bar

Slice the swiss roll or sponge and spread with jam. Arrange in a glass dish. Pour the sherry over —or use peach juice. Spoon drained peaches over. Whisk the thick cream until stiff. Gradually whisk in the thin cream or top-of-the-milk. Pour over the fruit and decorate with crushed chocolate flake.

Apple Meringue Flan

Preparation time: 5 minutes
Cooking time: grill about 5 minutes; oven 15-20 minutes
Special remarks: home-made sponge flans are quickly made using a swiss roll mixture
For 4 servings

1 bought sponge flan or baked pastry
  flan case
1 can apple pie filling or thick apple
  sauce
2 egg whites
4 level tablespoons caster sugar

Place flan on an ovenproof plate and fill with apple filling (or other chosen fruit). Whisk egg whites until stiff then whisk in half sugar—do not overwhisk. Fold in remaining sugar and pile on the fruit. Brown under a moderate grill or bake in a moderate oven, 350°F or Gas Mark 5.

Stewed Apples

1. If you like stewed apples with big chunks of apple: pare, core and slice 4 cooking apples. Mix ¼ pint water and 3-4 ounces sugar in a saucepan. Heat slowly to dissolve sugar. Drop apple slices into the hot syrup. Cover and simmer until tender, about 8 minutes. Additional flavourings are a dash of mace, cinnamon, ground cloves or lemon rind.

Apple Sauce

2. To make speedy apple sauce: pare, quarter and core 4 cooking apples. In saucepan mix apples and about ¼ pint water. Cover the pan and simmer until apples are soft. Mash apples to a smooth consistency with a potato masher. Finally stir in 3-4 ounces sugar and beat well.

Oil Pastry

1. For an 8 or 9-inch double-crust pie, sift 8 ounces plain flour and a teaspoon of salt into a large mixing bowl. Beat 5 tablespoons good quality cooking oil and 2 tablespoons cold water thoroughly together. Add all at once to the flour and stir together quickly with a fork.

2. Form dough into a ball; divide in half; flatten each slightly.
  Roll each piece on a well-floured board or between 2 pieces of greaseproof paper. The usual thickness is about ⅛ inch—take care not to pull or stretch the dough.

3. Peel off top sheet of paper and fit dough, paper side up, into pie plate. Remove remaining piece of paper. Trim edges even with rim of pie plate.
  Place top crust over the filled pie; trim off pastry edge even with rim. Seal edges with fork, or flute. Cut slits in top crust.

Saucy Baked Apples

Preparation time: 5 minutes
Cooking time: 30-40 minutes
Special remarks: choose a cooking apple
with a firm texture, e.g. Bramleys
For 4 servings

4 medium cooking apples
a few sultanas, dates or raisins
3 tablespoons golden syrup
3 tablespoons water
2 ounces butter

Wash apples and remove cores with a potato peeler or apple corer. With a sharp knife make a shallow cut through the skin, all round each apple. Stuff apples with a few sultanas, dates or raisins and arrange in baking dish.

Heat the syrup, water and butter in a small saucepan. When melted pour over the apples. Bake the apples in a hot oven, 400°F or Gas Mark 6. Baste frequently with syrup during the cooking. Test apples with a skewer or knife. For a neat appearance remove the top skin as in the photograph. Serve glazed with the cooking syrup.

Pineapple Croûtes

Preparation time: 5 minutes
Cooking time: 6 minutes
Special remarks: alternatively try lightly
poached thick apple rings
For 4 servings

8 thin slices bread
butter for spreading
4 rings canned pineapple
little apricot jam
2 eggs
1 dessertspoon sugar
¼ pint milk
butter and oil, for frying

Stack slices of bread together and cut into rounds the size of pineapple ring. Spread with butter. Put a ring of pineapple on a round of bread and fill centre with jam. Top with a second round of bread and butter. Beat eggs, sugar and milk on a plate and dip each croûte into the mixture on each side. Fry in hot oil and butter until golden, then fry other side. Serve very hot sprinkled with sugar.

Ribbon Sundae

Preparation time: 10 minutes
Cooking time: nil
Special remarks: any type of soft fruit may
be used, e.g. strawberries, raspberries
For 4 servings

1 (1-pint) carton strawberry instant dessert
½ pint milk
1 (4-5-ounce) strawberry flavoured yoghurt
few drops vanilla essence
1 (medium) can strawberries

Prepare instant dessert according to packet directions, but using only ½ pint milk; beat until smooth, fold in the yoghurt, and vanilla essence, if liked.

Drain the can of fruit, reserving juice. Chop the fruit or it may be puréed in the electric liquidiser. Add enough of the juice to make purée soft but not too moist. Spoon alternate layers of instant dessert and fruit in tall glasses—see illustration.

American Orange Flan

Preparation time: about 30 minutes not including jelly setting time
Cooking time: 8 minutes
Special remarks: this glamorous dessert takes a little preparation time but will bring glowing praise from family and friends
For 4-6 servings

GINGERNUT CRUST:
   24 ginger nuts (about 8 ounces)
   1 level tablespoon caster sugar
   3 ounces butter, melted
FILLING:
   1 orange jelly
   1 (large) can orange segments
   1 (small) can evaporated milk, chilled
   squeeze lemon juice
   whipped fresh cream and orange
      segment, to decorate

Crust: put all but 8 of the biscuits in a strong paper bag and crush until fine with a rolling pin. Mix with the butter and sugar. Press into bottom and sides of a buttered 8 or 9-inch pie plate. Bake in a moderate oven, 350°F or Gas Mark 4, for 8 minutes. Cool.

Drain juice from orange segments and make up to ½ pint if necessary with water. Put jelly in a small saucepan with half the juice and water. Heat until jelly dissolves but *do not* allow to boil. Add jelly to remaining juice and water. Stir well and chill until it becomes syrupy and begins to set.

Meanwhile whisk the evaporated milk with a squeeze of lemon juice until very thick. Fold most of the syrupy jelly (reserving some for glaze) into the whipped evaporated milk. Pour into prepared gingernut flan case. Arrange orange segments overlapping around edge of flan. Brush with remaining jelly glaze. Place halved ginger nuts around edge. Decorate with whipped cream and fresh orange twist.

Banana and Chocolate

Preparation time: 10 minutes and chilling time of 15 minutes
Cooking time: nil
Special remarks: this sweet may be prepared in advance
For 4 servings

   4 ripe bananas
   2 level tablespoons caster sugar
   ¼ pint thick cream, whipped
   vanilla essence
   juice of 1 lemon
   2 ounces chocolate, grated

Skin bananas and mash with a fork. Beat in the sugar until it dissolves. Fold in the cream, a few drops of vanilla essence and finally the lemon juice. Pour into individual dishes and chill. Decorate with grated chocolate.

A selection of fruit and cheeses is always popular for dessert

Fruit Cobbler

Preparation time: 10 minutes
Cooking time: 20-25 minutes
Special remarks: if you have time make a
plain scone mixture in usual way using
6 ounces flour
For 4 servings

1 can fruit (damsons, plums, rhubarb,
blackcurrants)
1 packet plain scone mix
1 egg, beaten
milk to mix

Pour fruit into a buttered deep ovenproof dish with half the juice. Make up scone mix according to packet directions adding sugar if required and egg and milk to mix; the dough should be fairly soft. Knead lightly on a floured board, roll out to $\frac{1}{2}$ inch in thickness. Cut out rounds with a $1\frac{1}{4}$-inch cutter. Place rings overlapping around the dish, leaving a space in the centre. Brush with milk and dredge with sugar. Bake in a hot oven, 425°F or Gas Mark 7, until topping is cooked and brown.

Choc-Orange Sponge

Preparation time: 15 minutes
Cooking time: 30-40 minutes
Special remarks: grease baking tins with
oil
For 4-6 servings

sponge mixture (see page 81)
1 level tablespoon cocoa
ORANGE CREAM:
1 egg
4 ounces sugar
2 teaspoons grated orange rind
2 tablespoons orange juice
1 teaspoon lemon juice
1 (4-5-ounce) carton thick cream
stiffly whipped

Prepare sponge mixture as for One-stage Sandwich Cake, but omit 1 level tablespoon flour and substitute the cocoa. Pour mixture into a greased and lined 6 or 7-inch square or oblong tin. Bake in a warm oven, 350°F or Gas Mark 3, until firm to the touch.

Meanwhile prepare orange cream: beat the egg in a small saucepan with sugar, orange rind and juices. Cook and stir over low heat until thick—about 5 minutes. Cool. When cold fold in whipped cream. Serve chilled.

Caramel Rice Pudding

Preparation time: 5 minutes
Cooking time: 10-15 minutes altogether
Special remarks: take care when making
caramel—it burns very easily
For 4 servings

3-4 bananas, peeled and sliced
3 ounces brown sugar
1 ounce butter
1 (large) can creamed rice pudding

Heat sugar and butter in a thick saucepan until it melts and turns golden brown, shaking pan frequently. Add bananas and cook over low heat until soft. Add the rice pudding and mix well. Pour into an ovenproof dish, dust with a little extra brown sugar and grill until sugar melts.

Ice Cream and Chocolate Sauce

Preparation time: 5 minutes
Cooking time: nil
*Special remarks: serve the chocolate
   sauce hot or cold*
For 4 servings

SAUCE:
   4 ounces drinking chocolate
   3 tablespoons boiling water
   ½ teaspoon vanilla essence
   1 family brick vanilla ice cream
   **3 ounces flaked toasted almonds or
   chopped walnuts**

Add the drinking chocolate to the boiling water. Beat thoroughly with a wooden spoon until smooth.

Arrange spoonfuls of ice cream in sundae glasses. Pour a little chocolate sauce over each serving. Sprinkle with flaked toasted nuts.

Cottage Soufflé

Preparation time: 10 minutes
Cooking time: about 30 minutes
*Special remarks: this light delicious
   pudding is a great favourite with every-
   one*
For 4 servings

   2 ounces butter
   1½ ounces flour
   ½ pint milk, boiling
   rind of 1 lemon
   2 ounces sugar
   3 eggs, separated
   4 tablespoons apricot jam
   1 ounce almonds, browned (optional)

Melt butter and add the flour. Stir in the boiling milk, lemon rind, sugar, egg yolks and a little lemon juice. Whisk egg whites stiffly and fold

into mixture. Pour into a 1-pint greased ovenproof dish and bake in a hot oven, 400°F or Gas Mark 6, until well risen. Pour the apricot jam heated with 1 tablespoon lemon juice over the pudding and sprinkle with browned almonds. Serve at once.

Dreamy Rice

Preparation time: 5 minutes
Cooking time: nil
*Special remarks: you can use any canned
   or fresh fruit for this dish*
For 4 servings

   1 packet dessert topping mix
   milk, see packet instructions
   1 (large) can creamed rice pudding
   1 (small) can prunes, stoned and drained

Empty the dessert topping mix into a basin, whisk with amount of milk stated on packet and whisk until mixture forms soft peaks—whisk for another minute. Combine with the rice pudding and chopped prunes. Serve piled in glasses.

Fruit Fritters

Preparation time: 15 minutes
Cooking time: about 5 minutes
Special remarks: you could use a packet of batter mix for the fritters but this French fritter batter is extra light and crisp
For 4 servings

Fruit—peeled and cored ½-inch thick slices of cooking apple; halved bananas or drained and dried canned pineapple rings
4 ounces plain flour
pinch salt
1 tablespoon cooking oil
¼ pint water
2 egg whites
cooking oil or white fat, for frying

Prepare fruit. Sieve flour and salt into a large bowl. Make a well in centre and using a wooden spoon work in the oil and half the water. Beat or whisk until smooth gradually adding rest of water. Beat well (the batter may be covered and stored at this stage in the refrigerator for up to 3 days).

Just before using whisk egg whites stiffly and fold quickly into batter. Heat about ½ inch oil or fat in a large frying pan. Test by dropping a teaspoonful of batter into fat—it should rise to the surface and turn golden brown in about half a minute. Skewer prepared fruit with a fork and dip into batter, drain off excess and place in the frying pan. Cook until golden brown on one side then fry other side. Don't fry too many fritters at once— they can be kept hot (uncovered) under a hot grill for a few minutes if necessary. Drain on crumpled kitchen or tissue paper and serve very hot sprinkled with sugar.

Cheesecake Pie

Preparation time: 20 minutes not including chilling time
Cooking time: 8 minutes
Special remarks: stale or broken sweet biscuits may be used for the biscuit crust
For 4-6 servings

BISCUIT CRUST:
6 ounces digestive biscuits
1 level tablespoon caster sugar
3 ounces butter
CHEESECAKE MIXTURE:
1 packet lemon pie filling
8 ounces cottage cheese, sieved
juice and finely grated rind of 1 small lemon
1 egg white
fresh strawberries
sugar

Put the biscuits in a strong paper bag and crush with a rolling pin. Put the butter and 1 tablespoon sugar in a saucepan and heat gently for a minute until butter melts. Add the biscuits, mix well and press into an 8 or 9-inch pie or flan dish. Bake in a moderate oven, 350°F or Gas Mark 4, for about 8 minutes. Cool.

Make up the lemon pie filling as directed on packet but use *half* the amount of water. Cool mixture and beat in the cottage cheese, lemon rind and juice. Now carefully fold in the stiffly whisked egg white. Decorate with sliced sweetened strawberries. Chill for 1-2 hours before serving.

Oriental Sundae

Preparation time: 5 minutes
Cooking time: 5 minutes
Special remarks: ice cream makes a quick delicious sweet with this special sauce
For 4-6 servings

1 can mandarin oranges
1½ level tablespoons cornflour
1 (small) can crushed pineapple

2 tablespoons orange marmalade
½ teaspoon ground ginger

Drain mandarin oranges reserving juice. Blend the juice with the cornflour in a small saucepan. Stir in the pineapple and juice, marmalade and ginger. Cook and stir over moderate heat until mixture boils and thickens. Stir in the mandarin oranges. Serve warm or cold over vanilla ice cream.

Chocolate Meringue

Preparation time: 10 minutes
Cooking time: brown under grill for 5-7 minutes
Special remarks: if you prefer a crisper meringue bake the pudding in a moderate oven, 350°F or Gas Mark 4, for 15-20 minutes
For 4 servings

2 ounces fine semolina
1 pint milk
2 rounded tablespoons drinking chocolate
6 ounces sugar
few drops almond essence
2 ounces butter
2 eggs, separated

Warm milk and sprinkle semolina (or ground rice) and drinking chocolate over the top. Bring to the boil and cook, stirring constantly, for 2 minutes. Remove from heat and beat in the sugar, butter, egg yolks and essence. Pour into a greased baking dish.

Whisk egg white until stiff, whisk in half the remaining sugar. Carefully fold in remaining sugar and pile this meringue on top of chocolate mixture. Brown under a moderate grill until golden.

Fruit Compote *(stewed fresh fruit)*

Preparation time: depends on type and size of fruit
Cooking time: depends on type and size of fruit
Special remarks: try stewing fruit this way to preserve all the flavour and texture
For 4 servings

3-4 ounces sugar (depending on tartness of fruit)
¼ pint water (½ pint for hard fruits)
strip of lemon peel
1 pound fresh fruit, prepared

Make a syrup by dissolving the sugar in the water over low heat. Once dissolved add the lemon peel and fruit, cover and simmer *slowly* until fruit is soft but still keeps its shape. Discard lemon peel.

A piece of cinnamon stick or 1 or 2 cloves add extra flavour to apples or pears.

> **TIME-SAVING TIP**
> Make custard the easy way—blend custard powder and a little milk in saucepan. Add rest of milk. Cook in usual way, stir in sugar.

Use Quick-mix pastry and a packet of lemon meringue pie filling, for this favourite sweet. Make it specially good by adding half the juice and the finely grated rind of 1 lemon with 1 extra tablespoon of sugar, to the filling.

Crispy Fruit Pudding

Preparation time: 10 minutes
Cooking time: 20-30 minutes
Special remarks: any plain sponge or fruit
*   cake crumbs may be used*
For 4 servings

6 ounces cake crumbs
2 ounces brown sugar
¼ teaspoon ground ginger
¼ teaspoon ground cinnamon
2 ounces butter
2 ounces sultanas, raisins, or dates,
   cleaned
grated rind and juice of 1 lemon
1 large cooking apple, peeled and grated

Crumble the cake crumbs into a mixing bowl. Add the brown sugar, ginger and cinnamon. Add the butter cut in small pieces. Finally mix in the dried fruit and lemon rind and juice. Mix everything lightly together. Line a greased pie dish with most of this mixture, add a layer of apples and then the rest of the cake crumb mixture. Bake until crisp in a hot oven, 400°F or Gas Mark 6. Serve with ice cream.

Fruit Crumble

Preparation time: 10 minutes
Cooking time: 30 minutes
Special remarks: alternatively use canned
*   apricots, peaches or plums but thicken*
*   the juice with 1 level tablespoon corn-*

flour and add 1 tablespoon sugar
1 can fruit pie filling
3 ounces margarine
6 ounces plain flour
1 level teaspoon mixed spice or
   cinnamon
3 ounces caster sugar
grated rind of 1 orange or lemon

Pour chosen fruit pie filling into greased baking dish. Sieve flour and spice into a mixing bowl. Rub the fat into the flour until mixture resembles fine breadcrumbs; stir in sugar and orange or lemon rind. Sprinkle on top of fruit and dust with extra sugar. Bake in a moderate oven, 350°F or Gas Mark 4.

Gingered Pears

Preparation time: 10 minutes
Cooking time: 10-15 minutes altogether
Special remarks: the cooking time depends
*   upon the ripeness of the fruit*
For 4 servings

4 ripe pears
1 large orange, rind and juice
1 lemon, rind and juice
1 ounce caster sugar
½ level teaspoon ground ginger

Pare the rind thinly from the orange and lemon into a small saucepan. Add the juice, sugar and ginger. Heat until sugar dissolves. Meanwhile peel, core and quarter the pears, put in a separate saucepan. Strain the ginger sauce over the pears, cover and cook over low heat until tender. Pour into serving dishes and serve warm or cold.

Quick Apple Charlotte

Preparation time: 10 minutes
Cooking time: 20-30 minutes
Special remarks: if you are not using
*   mincemeat add a few washed sultanas*
*   or raisins and ½ teaspoon mixed spice*
*   to the apples*
For 4 servings

about 8 slices brown or white bread
butter or margarine for spreading
1 can apple sauce or 4 medium apples,
   stewed
2 tablespoons mincemeat (optional)
1 tablespoon lemon juice
3 tablespoons golden syrup

¼ pint water
1 tablespoon brown sugar

Spread bread with butter or margarine; trim crusts if preferred. Cut slices in fingers and use about half to line a greased pie or baking dish. Mix apple sauce or stewed apples, mincemeat (if used) and lemon juice together. Pour into the centre of the lined dish. Cover with remaining slices of bread, buttered side up. Melt the golden syrup and water and pour carefully over the bread. Sprinkle with brown sugar. Bake in a hot oven until crisp and golden brown.

Fudge Mould

Preparation time: 10 minutes not including setting time
Cooking time: 5 minutes
Special remarks: children will love this sweet served with canned mandarin oranges
For 4 servings

2 ounces margarine
2 ounces cornflour
1 pint milk
4 level teaspoons golden syrup

Melt margarine in a saucepan. Remove from heat and blend in the cornflour using a wooden spoon. Gradually stir in the milk; mix well. Heat to boiling point and boil for 2 minutes, stirring constantly.

Heat syrup in a separate pan until a good brown colour. Beat into the sauce. Pour into a wetted mould and serve cold.

Quick to Make—Longer to Cook

This is the casserole section—full of dishes which are quick to prepare and can be left to cook on their own, sometimes for several hours.

Also in this section you will find complete meals using the automatic time control. Most modern gas and electric cookers are fitted with this control which means you prepare the food in advance, put it in the oven in the morning and set the controls. When you come home in the evening the meal is ready—perfectly cooked and ready to serve.

MENU 1
Hollywood Chicken Casserole
Baked Potatoes
Plum Crumble

Hollywood Chicken Casserole

Preparation time: 20 minutes
Cooking time: about 1-1¼ hours
Special remarks: all the dishes may be put in the oven at the same time and the auto-timer set. Put the potatoes and casserole on the top shelf and the pudding below
For 4 servings

1 (2½-3-pound) roasting chicken
   or 4 large chicken joints
3-4 tablespoons flour
1 teaspoon salt
¼ teaspoon pepper
paprika pepper
2-3 tablespoons oil, for frying
8 ounces small onions, peeled and left whole
2-3 medium carrots, scraped and chopped
1 can frozen orange juice concentrate, thawed
½ pint chicken stock or water
1 tablespoon brown sugar
¼ teaspoon ground ginger
½ tablespoon curry powder
4 ounces mushrooms, washed and sliced

Put the flour, salt, pepper and paprika in a strong paper bag—shake to mix. Add 2 or 3 pieces of chicken at a time and shake. (Reserve any left-over flour.) Fry chicken joints, skin side down first, in hot oil in a frying pan. Brown joints quickly, drain and place in a casserole. Fry the small onions until brown, adding more oil if necessary. Drain and add to the chicken with the carrots. Blend flour with oil in frying pan and stir in the orange juice and the stock or cold water. Cook and stir until mixture thickens and boils, add the sugar, ginger, curry powder and mushrooms. The sauce should be fairly thin—if necessary dilute with a little more stock or water. Pour over chicken, cover and cook in centre of a moderate oven, 355°F or Gas Mark 4, until chicken is tender.

Baked Potatoes

Choose even-sized old potatoes, scrub well, dry and prick. Brush with cooking oil or rub with lard or dripping. Put on the oven shelf and bake for about 1 hour—they should feel soft when pinched. Cut a cross in the top of each potato, squeeze and put in a knob of butter.

Plum Crumble

Drain a medium can of plums and mix the juice with 2 level tablespoons cornflour. Pour into an ovenproof baking dish. Prepare crumble topping by rubbing 4 ounces butter or margarine into 6 ounces plain flour. Add 2 ounces caster sugar and sprinkle over the fruit. Press down lightly and sprinkle with extra sugar. Bake for about 1 hour beneath the chicken casserole. Serve hot with custard.

```
●●●●●●●●●●●●●●●●●●●●●●●●●●●●●●●
●                                               ●
●                  MENU 2                       ●
●               Roast Pork                      ●
●         Roast Potatoes and Onions             ●
●           Apple Sauce and Gravy               ●
●               Braised Celery                  ●
●           French-style Rice Pudding           ●
●                                               ●
●●●●●●●●●●●●●●●●●●●●●●●●●●●●●●●
```

In this menu the complete meal can be cooked in the oven at the same time without attention. It is the ideal menu for the auto-timer, as it can be left all day if necessary. Try this menu too if you are going to be busy all day and want to forget about cooking—it can be left quite happily to cook itself! Before serving make a gravy from the roast pork drippings.

Roast Pork Dinner

Special remarks: set time control to 1 hour 45 minutes cooking time. Set the oven thermostat to a hot oven, 400°F or Gas Mark 6
For 4 servings

1 (2½-3-pound) pork loin, spare ribs or leg
salt
1½-2 pounds potatoes, peeled and halved
oil for brushing
2-3 large onions, peeled and halved
APPLE SAUCE:
2 large cooking apples, peeled and sliced
2 tablespoons water
2 tablespoons sugar
knob of butter

To obtain crisp crackling rub salt into the scored pork skin before roasting. Put the meat, preferably on a rack, in the roasting tin. Brush the potatoes with oil. Arrange potatoes and onions beneath the rack in the roasting tin. Put on top shelf of oven.

APPLE SAUCE: slice apples into a baking dish. Sprinkle with sugar and water. Dot with butter and cover closely with aluminium foil. Put on bottom shelf of oven.

BRAISED CELERY: scrub and trim 4 small heads of celery. Tie into shape. Fry lightly in a little butter until golden brown. Put in an oven-proof dish with enough stock to come half-way up the celery. Sprinkle with salt, pepper and a little

butter. Cover and cook on a shelf below the roast pork.

French-style Rice Pudding

Preparation time: 5 minutes
Special remarks: leave the pudding in the oven while you finish and serve the first course as it will take a little longer to cook
For 4 servings

1½ ounces short grain (Carolina) rice
1 pint milk, boiling
1 ounce butter
pinch salt
1 egg, beaten
2 ounces sugar
little grated nutmeg

Wash rice in cold water and put in a buttered ovenproof dish. Stir in the boiling milk. Add the butter and stir until it melts then add the salt, sugar and egg mixing well. Sprinkle with nutmeg and bake on the bottom shelf.

When you're making a mix-in-one-bowl main dish, combine it in the casserole to save effort, and washing-up too!

Two Good Hearty Casseroles

Sweet 'n Sour Casserole

Preparation time: 15 minutes
Cooking time: 2 hours
Special remarks: stewing steak could be used instead of rump
Serving suggestions: boiled buttered noodles
For 4 servings

1 ounce fat
2 onions, chopped
1 pound rump steak
seasoned flour
½ pint stock
1 tablespoon brown sugar
2 tablespoons wine vinegar
1 teaspoon Worcester sauce
¼ teaspoon ground ginger
1 bay leaf
extra salt and pepper to taste
8 ounces noodles

Brown onions in hot fat. Cut the steak in cubes and coat with seasoned flour. Remove onions from fat and brown meat quickly. Add the stock and all remaining ingredients. Bring to boiling, stirring constantly. Cover closely and cook in a moderate oven, 350°F or Gas Mark 4, until tender. Remove bay leaf before serving. Ten minutes before serving boil the noodles in plenty of boiling salted water. Drain and add a knob of butter.

Lamb Stew 'n Dumplings

Preparation time: 15 minutes
Cooking time: 2 hours
Special remarks: this stew is complete with vegetables and dumplings
For 4 servings

1½-2 pounds stewing lamb
1 ounce dripping or lard
2 level tablespoons flour
1 teaspoon paprika
2 teaspoons salt
¼ teaspoon pepper
½ pint stock or water
1 (medium) can tomato juice
1 clove garlic, crushed (optional)
¼ teaspoon rosemary, crushed
2 carrots peeled and sliced
6 small whole onions or 1 large onion, sliced
1 medium potato, peeled
1 (medium) can broad beans
DUMPLINGS:
8 ounces self-raising flour
½ teaspoon salt
½ teaspoon mixed dried herbs
3 ounces suet, shredded
water to mix

Cut the lamb into large cubes, trimming off the excess fat. Combine flour, paprika, salt and pepper and toss meat in this seasoned flour. Heat fat in a frying pan and brown meat well on all sides—takes about 10 minutes. Remove from pan and place in the base of a large casserole. Drain fat from frying pan and add the stock or water, tomato juice, crushed garlic and rosemary, scraping with a wooden spoon to remove crusty sediment. Pour this sauce over the meat. Stir in the carrots, onions and roughly chopped potato. Cover and cook in a moderate oven, 350°F or Gas Mark 4, for about 2 hours. Alternatively simmer the casserole on top of the stove until lamb is tender. Stir in the drained broad beans.

Twenty-five minutes before serving time make the dumplings. Sift flour and salt into a basin. Add herbs and suet. Using a knife, stir in enough cold water to make a soft, almost sticky dough. Flour hands and divide dough into small balls. Drop dumplings into the simmering stew, cover and cook for 15 minutes.

Mushroom Meat Loaf

Preparation time: 10 minutes
Cooking time: 1¼ hours
Special remarks: this complete meal can be put in the oven at the same time and left to cook unattended
Serving suggestions: crisscross baked potatoes; date stuffed apples and cream
For 4-6 servings

1 can mushrooms, chopped
1 egg, slightly beaten
1½ teaspoons Worcester sauce
salt and pepper
½ teaspoon dry mustard
1 large onion, grated
6 ounces fresh breadcrumbs
stock, to mix (about ¼ pint)
1 pound minced steak
4 ounces sausage meat } minced together
4 ounces bacon
1 tablespoon tomato paste or ketchup
1 tablespoon cooking oil
grilled mushroom caps, to garnish
strips of canned pimiento, to garnish

In a large mixing bowl put the mushrooms (and liquid), egg, Worcester sauce, seasonings, onion and breadcrumbs. Add enough stock to make a soft consistency. Beat well together and leave to stand for 5 minutes. Stir in the minced steak, sausage meat and bacon, mix lightly but thoroughly. Press mixture into a loaf tin or shape into a loaf and bake in a roasting tin. Cover with aluminium foil and bake in a moderate oven, 350°F or Gas Mark 4, for 1 hour. Mix tomato paste or ketchup and cooking oil, brush over meat loaf. Bake a further 15 minutes to glaze. Garnish with mushroom caps and pimiento strips.

Crisscross Baked Potatoes

Preparation time: 5 minutes
Cooking time: 1¼ hours
*Special remarks: bake the potatoes on the
    same shelf as the meat loaf and sprinkle
    with paprika when you glaze the meat.*
2-3 medium potatoes, scrubbed
2 ounces butter or margarine, melted
salt and pepper
paprika pepper

Halve potatoes lengthwise. Make diagonal cuts
about ⅛ inch deep, forming a crisscross pattern.
Brush cut surfaces with melted fat and sprinkle
with salt and pepper. Arrange on a baking sheet.

Date Stuffed Apples

Core and peel a strip from top of each cooking
apple. Stuff apples with dates and chopped walnuts. Sprinkle each apple with sugar and 1 tablespoon water. Top with a knob of butter and bake
uncovered for about 1 hour, below the meat loaf
and potatoes.

Spaghetti Supper

Preparation time: 5 minutes
Cooking time: 1 hour
*Special remarks: you can of course use a
    shallow flameproof casserole or frying
    pan for all the electric frying pan recipes*
For 4-6 servings

1 pound minced steak
2 medium onions, chopped
1 clove garlic, crushed
1 (15-ounce) can peeled tomatoes
1 (6-ounce) can tomato concentrate
    (paste)
¾ pint stock or water
1 tablespoon chilli powder
salt and freshly ground black pepper
1 teaspoon sugar
1 teaspoon oregano or pimento
8 ounces spaghetti, broken
onion rings and/or 1 green pepper, to
    garnish
Parmesan cheese, grated

Heat electric frying pan to about 380°F, add
minced steak and brown quickly, breaking it up
with a wooden spoon. Stir in onions, garlic,
tomatoes, tomato concentrate, stock or water,
chilli powder, seasoning, sugar and oregano.
Cover and heat to boiling; reduce heat (220°F)
and simmer for 30 minutes, stirring occasionally.
Add the spaghetti and stir to separate strands.
Simmer, covered, a further 30 minutes or until
spaghetti is tender. Stir frequently. Add the
onions and green pepper rings 10 minutes before
cooking time is completed. Sprinkle with grated
Parmesan cheese and serve with French bread.

CHAPTER 6

Frypan Cookery

The electric frying pan can save you time and trouble. You can mix, cook and sometimes even serve—*all from one pan*. Tempting casseroles, super sandwiches, and even desserts and cakes can be made in the pan.

Toasted Chicken Sandwiches

Preparation time: 10 minutes
Cooking time: 7 minutes
Special remarks: use the electric frying pan to make delicious toasted sand-wiches—excellent for snack meals
For 4 servings

2 ounces butter
8 slices bread
2 eggs, beaten
¼ pint milk
salt and pepper
leftover diced, cooked chicken (about 1½ cups)
8 thin slices Cheddar cheese
1 small can asparagus spears, drained (optional)

Preheat electric frying pan to hot (400°F). Melt the butter. Beat eggs and milk together in a large shallow plate or dish. Add salt and pepper to taste. Dip 4 slices of bread quickly on both sides in beaten egg mixture. Place the 4 slices in heated frying pan. Divide chicken and cheese between the 4 slices bread and top with asparagus spears. Dip the remaining 4 slices bread in egg and milk

mixture adding extra milk if necessary. Cover the filling with the bread. Using a fish slice press the sandwich firmly together. Cook until brown on one side then turn over and brown other side. Serve hot garnished with pineapple slices which can be heated in the electric frying pan alongside the sandwiches.

German Potato Salad

Preparation time: 10 minutes
Cooking time: 10 minutes altogether
Special remarks: try this tasty hot potato salad—it will add flavour and zest to any cold meat
For 4-6 servings

4-6 medium potatoes, boiled in their jackets
6 slices bacon, chopped
1 medium onion, grated or finely chopped
1 (10½-ounce) can celery soup
5 tablespoons milk
salt and pepper
2 tablespoons sweet chutney or pickle
1 tablespoon vinegar
1 hardboiled egg

Preheat electric frying pan to hot (380°F). Dice the cooked potatoes. Fry the chopped bacon until cooked then remove. Drain off all but about 2 tablespoons bacon fat. Add the onion and cook for 3 minutes or until soft. Stir in the soup, milk, seasoning, chutney or pickle and vinegar. Cook and stir until mixture boils. Carefully stir in the potatoes and most of the bacon. Lower heat and simmer for a few minutes to heat potatoes. Sprinkle with remaining bacon and garnish with parsley and wedges of hardboiled egg.

Skillet Baked Bacon or Gammon

Preparation time: soaking time plus 10 minutes
Cooking time: allow 20 minutes per pound and 20 minutes over
Special remarks: a large joint cooked in this way will save you time by giving you several good meals from one joint
Serving suggestions: glazed potatoes and bananas; mixed green salad or green vegetable

1 piece of bacon or gammon
¼ pint cider
4 tablespoons warmed syrup
1 teaspoon dry mustard
pinch ground cloves or 3-4 whole cloves
potatoes, parboiled
bananas
flour and brown sugar

Cover the joint with cold water and soak for 1 hour. Weigh the joint and calculate cooking time. Put in a saucepan, cover with fresh cold water and bring slowly to the boil, skimming away any scum. Time the cooking from now—allowing *half* the cooking, i.e. if joint weighs 6 pounds cook for only 1 hour 10 minutes. Cover and simmer gently. Drain and cut off the rind, score fat into diamond shapes.

Heat electric frying pan to fairly hot (350°F). Put the joint in the pan and pour the cider over. Brush with the warmed syrup. Put lid on pan (air vents closed) and cook for remainder of time. 15 minutes before cooking time is completed mix equal quantities of flour and brown sugar with the ground cloves and mustard on a plate. Roll the potatoes and bananas in the mixture and add potatoes to the pan. Sprinkle any remaining flour and sugar over the joint. Do not cover. Add bananas a few minutes before serving.

Fruity Pork Chops

Preparation time: 5 minutes
Cooking time: 30-35 minutes altogether
Special remarks: these chops can be left to cook unattended while you prepare the rest of the meal
Serving suggestions: sauté potatoes; green salad
For 4 servings

4 pork chops, about ¾ inch thick
seasoned flour
butter or bacon fat for frying
1 tablespoon cornflour
1 medium onion, grated or finely chopped
salt and freshly ground black pepper
½ pint cider
1 (medium) can fruit cocktail

Preheat electric frying pan to fairly hot (360°F). Trim excess fat from pork chops using scissors. Snip fat edge of the meat to prevent curling. Dip in seasoned flour. Heat fat and brown chops thoroughly on both sides—about 15 minutes. Stir in the cornflour blended with the cider, onion and seasoning. When boiling reduce heat (220°F), cover and simmer until tender. Five minutes before serving add the fruit cocktail and enough juice to make the sauce of a pouring consistency.

SECTION TWO
Snack Meals

Preparing and cooking snack meals at odd times of the day and evening is often a source of great worry to the housewife. In this section you will find quick, easy recipes for all types of snack meals—brunches, lunches, television snacks, high teas and suppers.

CHAPTER 7

Brunch and Weekend Breakfast Menus

Brunch—a very late breakfast which runs into lunch—is becoming very popular for weekends and holidays. It also serves as an excellent opportunity for a weekend party meal.

BRUNCH MENU 1

Raisin Stuffed Apples

Preparation time: 5 minutes
Cooking time: 15 minutes
Special remarks: if serving the apples cold omit butter
For 6 servings

6 large cooking apples
6 ounces brown sugar
6 ounces seedless raisins
butter
generous ¼ pint water

Core apples and cut a strip from top of each. Mix brown sugar and raisins and fill each apple with a little of the mixture. Dot with butter. Place apples in a large saucepan; add water. Cover tightly and heat to boiling. Lower heat and simmer until tender—about 15 minutes. Serve warm or cold.

Corn Meal Fritters with Gammon and Eggs

Preparation time: 15 minutes
Cooking time: ham 10-15 minutes; eggs 3 minutes; to fry corn fritters 5-10 minutes
Special remarks: prepare corn fritters the night before required
For 6 servings

CORN MEAL FRITTERS:
1 pint plus 4 tablespoons water
4 ounces corn meal
scant ½ pint cold water

1 teaspoon salt
1 teaspoon sugar
GAMMON AND EGGS:
  6 ¼-inch thick gammon rashers
  oil for cooking
  6 eggs

Corn fritters: heat the larger amount of water to boiling in a saucepan. Gradually add remaining ingredients, stirring constantly. Cook until mixture thickens. Cover and continue cooking over *low* heat, for 10-15 minutes. Pour in a loaf tin. Cool. Chill overnight. Slice ½-inch thick and fry until golden in hot fat, turning once.

Gammon and eggs: cut rind from gammon with scissors and snip fat at intervals. Put rashers on greased grid of grill pan and brush with oil or melted fat. Grill under medium heat for 5 minutes. Turn, baste with fat and continue grilling until tender.

A minute or two before gammon is ready, fry the eggs in a little hot fat. Baste with the fat while cooking. When eggs are just set remove from pan with a fish slice and serve on a hot platter with the gammon and corn meal fritters. Serve with crisp rolls or muffins.

BRUNCH MENU 2

Breakfast Bowl

  Preparation time: 5 minutes
  Cooking time: nil
  Special remarks: raspberries and sliced banana are delicious too; or try prunes and fresh sliced orange

For 4 servings
  1 small can pineapple chunks
  fresh strawberries, about 12 ounces
  3-4 tablespoons sugar

Drain pineapple reserving juice. Chop the chunks if they are very large. Mix pineapple and sliced strawberries carefully in a bowl. Sprinkle with sugar and pour pineapple juice over.

Easy Scrambled Eggs 'n Ham

  Preparation time: 5 minutes
  Cooking time: ham or gammon 15 minutes (if very thick allow 15-20 minutes); scrambled eggs about 5 minutes
  Special remarks: this delicious brunch should summon the sleepiest member of the family!
  For 4 servings

  4 ¼- or ½-inch thick gammon rashers
  or 1 large thick gammon steak
  2 ounces butter
  6 eggs
  6 tablespoons milk
  salt and pepper

See previous recipe for cooking of gammon or ham. If you are using a large thick gammon steak allow a longer cooking time.

Put butter in a saucepan. Drop in each egg. Add milk and seasoning. Place over *moderate* heat and using a wooden spoon combine (don't beat) eggs. Stir gently until mixture thickens and is just set.

CHAPTER 8

Lunches, Suppers and High Teas

The recipes in this chapter are all very simple and quick to prepare. They solve the problem of what to serve when the family want a quick, tasty and filling snack.

Ham Scramble

Preparation time: 5 minutes
Cooking time: 5 minutes
Special remarks: this makes an excellent television snack or late-night supper
For 4 servings

6 ounces cooked ham, chopped
2 ounces butter
6 eggs
6 tablespoons milk
salt and pepper
4 packets potato crisps or straws

Melt butter in a strong saucepan. Beat eggs lightly with milk and seasoning. Pour into saucepan and stir slowly over *gentle* heat until mixture thickens and becomes creamy—do not overcook. Remove from heat and stir in the chopped ham. Serve surrounded by potato crisps or straws.

Mexican Mix-up

Preparation time: 5 minutes
Cooking time: 30-35 minutes
Special remarks: to skin sausages more easily soak in cold water for 5 minutes
For 4 servings

1 pound sausages, skinned
1 onion, chopped
1 green pepper, de-seeded and sliced
4-6 ounces quick-cooking macaroni
1 tablespoon sugar
salt and freshly ground black pepper
1 level teaspoon chilli powder
1 (15-ounce) can tomatoes
1 tablespoon tomato concentrate (paste)
$\frac{1}{4}$ pint stock
1 small carton sour cream or yoghurt
grated cheese, to serve

Halve then brown sausages in a shallow casserole over moderate heat. Pour off excess fat and add onion and green pepper to sausages. Cook until tender. Stir in macaroni and next 5 ingredients. Cover and simmer until macaroni is cooked, stirring occasionally. Stir in sour cream or yoghurt; heat but do not boil. Serve with grated cheese.

Rice Cream

Preparation time: 10 minutes
Cooking time: nil
Special remarks: plump the raisins by heating in 4 tablespoons water and a little lemon juice for about 5 minutes. Drain
For 4 servings

2 ounces raisins, plumped (see above)
1 (15½-ounce) can creamed rice
dash nutmeg
1 (6-ounce) can dairy cream
2 ounces walnuts, chopped
2 teaspoons instant coffee powder (optional)
4 whole walnuts, for decoration

Mix the plumped raisins, rice, nutmeg and chopped walnuts. Shake the can of cream until thick. Turn out and add instant coffee powder. Carefully fold most of the cream into the rice mixture. Spoon remaining cream on top and decorate with a walnut half. If possible, serve chilled.

Luncheon Beano

Preparation time: 10 minutes
Cooking time: grill—10 minutes or oven—20 minutes
Special remarks: children will love this appetising and nourishing lunch dish
Serving suggestions: hot French bread; green or tomato salad
For 4 servings

1 (12-ounce) can luncheon meat
a little made mustard
1 (15-ounce) can baked beans
2 tablespoons brown sauce
1 small onion, grated
4 ounces Cheddar cheese, grated

Cut luncheon meat into 8 slices. Spread a little made mustard on each slice, if liked. Fry in hot fat or oil until slightly browned on each side—about 5 minutes. Meanwhile combine the baked beans, brown sauce and onion in a saucepan; heat to boiling. Drain luncheon meat and arrange around inner edge of an ovenproof baking dish. Pour bean mixture in centre and sprinkle with cheese. Brown under a moderate grill for 10 minutes or in a fairly hot oven, 375°F or Gas Mark 5, for 20 minutes.

TIME-SAVING TIP
Peel and trim vegetables onto their wrapping paper. This can be rolled up and thrown away—no mess on the kitchen table!

Special Cauliflower Cheese

Preparation time: 15 minutes
Cooking time: 20 minutes altogether
Special remarks: use fresh or dried bread-
crumbs for the crispy topping
For 4 servings

1 large cauliflower
2½ ounces butter or margarine
2 ounces flour
1 pint milk
6 ounces cheese, grated
salt and pepper
6 rashers lean bacon, rind removed
2-3 ounces white breadcrumbs

Trim outer leaves from the cauliflower. Cut into quarters, removing coarse thick stalks. Cook, stem side down, in fast boiling salted water until tender —about 10-15 minutes. Pour off ¼ pint cooking liquid. Drain cauliflower and arrange in a baking dish. Meanwhile fry the bacon until crisp, drain and chop. Melt the butter or margarine, stir in the flour and cook 2-3 minutes. Remove from heat and add the ¼ pint cooking liquid and the milk. Bring to the boil and continue to stir until sauce thickens. Remove from heat and add seasoning, fried bacon and most of grated cheese. Pour sauce over cauliflower. Sprinkle with remaining cheese mixed with breadcrumbs. Brown under a hot grill.

Loch Fyne Savoury

Preparation time: 10 minutes
Cooking time: 15 minutes
Special remarks: brush mushrooms under
running water, drain and dry
For 4 servings

4 fillets smoked haddock
½ pint milk
¼ pint water
8 ounces mushrooms, washed and
   sliced
1 tablespoon parsley, chopped
2 ounces butter
little pepper
mashed potatoes, to serve

Wash the fish, dry immediately. Put the fillets in a shallow saucepan and add milk, water and a dash of pepper. Bring to the boil, reduce heat and add mushrooms. Simmer for 10 minutes or until fish is cooked. Lift fish from pan with a fish slice or draining spoon onto a hot serving platter. Cover and keep warm. Add butter and parsley to mushrooms and milk. Cook briskly (uncovered) until liquid is reduced and slightly thickened. Pour over fish and serve with hot mashed potatoes.

Beef Potato Salad

Preparation time: 10 minutes
Cooking time: potatoes—20-25 minutes
Special remarks: try this hearty, tangy potato salad using new potatoes, in season
For 4 servings

8 small potatoes, scrubbed but not peeled
DRESSING:
4 tablespoons mayonnaise or salad cream
2 tablespoons milk
½ teaspoon celery seed
½ teaspoon mustard seed
1 teaspoon sugar
½ teaspoon salt

½-1 tablespoon chopped piccalilly (optional)
1 small onion
¼ large cabbage
few spring onions
1 (12-ounce) can corned beef

Put the potatoes in boiling, salted water and simmer until just tender.

Meanwhile in a large bowl mix together all the ingredients for the dressing. Grate or chop the onion very finely. Wash the cabbage and shred finely. Wash the spring (green) onions and chop. Cut the corned beef into cubes.

When potatoes are tender, peel while still hot. Cube and mix carefully with dressing. Add onion, cabbage, spring onions and corned beef, mix carefully so potatoes are not broken up. Serve warm or cold.

Gourmet Pancake Rolls

Preparation time: 10 minutes
Cooking time: 30 minutes altogether
Special remarks: if possible, allow batter
mixture to rest in a cool place for 30
minutes before using
For 6 servings

BATTER:
 4 ounces plain flour
 good pinch salt
 1 large egg
 ¼ pint milk
 ¼ pint water
FILLING:
 4-6 ounces cooked chicken, minced or
  finely chopped
 1 (small) can spinach, well-drained
 1 (10-ounce) can condensed cream of
  chicken soup
 2 ounces Parmesan cheese, grated
 1 small onion, grated
 salt and pepper
 scant ½ pint milk
 few sliced almonds, optional

Batter: sieve flour and salt into a bowl. Make a well in centre and add the egg and 2 tablespoons milk. Beat together, gradually drawing in the flour from the sides of bowl. Add remaining milk and water slowly, beating between each addition. Melt a little oil in a strong frying pan and heat until smoking hot. Pour 3-4 tablespoons batter into pan; lift pan and tilt so batter covers base thinly. Brown pancake on one side only. Slide out, keep hot and make remaining pancakes.
Filling: mix chicken, spinach, *half* the soup, cheese, onion and seasoning. Spoon a heaped tablespoon filling on unbrowned side of each pancake; roll up. Arrange seam side down in a shallow greased baking dish. Combine soup with milk and pour over pancakes. Sprinkle with almonds. Bake

in a moderate oven, 350°F or Gas Mark 4, until lightly browned.

Tossed Chicken Salad

Preparation time: 10 minutes
Cooking time: nil
Special remarks: serve salads throughout
the year varying the ingredients ac-
cording to season
For 4 servings

 1 lettuce, washed
 ½ bunch watercress, washed
 2 tomatoes, cut in wedges
 ½ cucumber, sliced
 few spring onions, chopped
 2 ounces black olives
 1 dessert apple
 cold cooked chicken (about 12 ounces)
 1 hardboiled egg cut in wedges
 2 ounces cheese, finely grated
FRENCH DRESSING:
 ¼ teaspoon salt
 pinch pepper
 ¼ teaspoon dry mustard
 ¼ teaspoon sugar
 1 tablespoon lemon juice
 3 tablespoons olive or salad oil

Prepare salad ingredients. Break lettuce into salad bowl, add watercress leaves, tomatoes, cucumber, spring onions and olives. Mix together.

Put the dressing ingredients in a screwtop jar, place cap on jar and shake well. Pour over salad ingredients.

Chop but do not peel the apple and add to the salad with the chicken. Toss everything together thoroughly with salad servers. Garnish with wedges of hardboiled egg and finely grated cheese.

Poached Eggs Suprême

Preparation time: 10 minutes
Cooking time: about 5 minutes
Special remarks: the eggs may be poached
   in the sauce
For 4 servings

1 medium onion, grated or finely
   chopped
1 ounce butter or margarine
1 (small) can cream of chicken soup
salt, pepper and nutmeg
5 tablespoons milk
4 eggs
rounds of bread or rolls
chopped parsley

Cook the onion in hot butter or margarine until soft but not brown. Stir in chicken soup, seasoning and milk. Heat gently. Poach the eggs separately in water, or in the sauce.

Toast the bread or rolls and butter them. To serve: place a drained poached egg on bread. Spoon sauce over and sprinkle with chopped parsley.

Hot Cheese Sandwich

Preparation time: 5 minutes
Cooking time: 3-4 minutes
Special remarks: to make the sandwich
   extra good add a slice of cooked ham or
gammon, below the cheese
For 4 servings

4 thick slices bread, toasted
butter for spreading
2 tablespoons chutney or sweet pickle
4 slices cheese
4 rings pineapple, drained

Spread toast with butter. Spread with a thin layer of chutney or sweet pickle. Top with a slice of cheese and pineapple ring. Grill until cheese is melted.

Corned Beef Burgers

Preparation time: 5 minutes
Cooking time: 10-15 minutes
Special remarks: easy to make and serve—
* burgers are always popular*
For 6 servings

6 rolls or bread buns
1 (6-ounce) can corned beef
4 ounces Cheddar cheese, grated
2 tablespoons tomato ketchup or sauce
good dash Worcester sauce

Split rolls or bread buns and remove soft insides.
Chop the corned beef and mix with the cheese,
ketchup and Worcester sauce. Mix thoroughly.
Fill rolls with the filling. Bake in a hot oven, 400°F
or Gas Mark 6, for 10-15 minutes or until heated
through.

Lamb Patties

Preparation time: 10 minutes
Cooking time: 20 minutes altogether
Special remarks: serve patties with a
* green salad. Alternatively use ham-*
* burger recipe with minced meat (see*
* page 28)*
For 6 servings

12 ounces cooked lamb, minced
1 onion, grated
salt and pepper
1 teaspoon curry powder
1 egg, beaten
2 ounces breadcrumbs
squeeze lemon juice
1 (4-serving) packet instant potato
milk (see packet)
1 tomato, cut in wedges
2 ounces cheese, grated (optional)

Mix together the meat, onion, seasoning, curry
powder, egg, breadcrumbs and lemon juice.
Shape into 6 patties. Place in a shallow baking
dish. Cover and bake in a hot oven, 400°F or Gas
Mark 6.
  Meanwhile prepare mashed potato according
to packet directions; add a little extra milk to make
it soft.
  Top each patty with a spoonful of mashed
potato. Add a wedge of tomato and sprinkle with
cheese, if used. Bake in a hot oven, 400°F or Gas
Mark 6, until hot—about 10 minutes.

Suppertime Hash

Preparation time: 15 minutes
Cooking time: 30 minutes altogether
Special remarks: choose this recipe for an
* easy fork supper*
For 4 servings

1 tablespoon oil
1 medium onion, chopped
1 stalk celery, chopped
2 rashers bacon, chopped
1 clove garlic, crushed
1 (15-ounce) can peeled tomatoes
1 tablespoon tomato concentrate (paste)
2 teaspoons sugar
¼ pint stock
2 teaspoons Worcester sauce
1 pound lean cooked meat, cubed
salt and pepper
few cooked chopped potatoes (about
  1 cupful)
4-6 salted cracker biscuits
1 ounce margarine or butter, melted

Heat oil and add chopped onion, celery, bacon and
garlic. Cover pan and sweat vegetables over low
heat for 10 minutes, stirring occasionally. Stir in
the can of tomatoes, juice, tomato paste, sugar,
stock, Worcester sauce and seasoning. Carefully
stir in the cooked meat and potatoes. Heat to
boiling. Tip into an ovenproof baking dish. Crush
the cracker crumbs and stir into the butter or
margarine which has been melted in a small
saucepan. Sprinkle around meat mixture. Bake uncovered in a fairly hot oven, 375°F or Gas Mark 5,
until crisp and bubbling.

CHAPTER 9

Hot and Hearty Sandwiches

Here are lots of ideas for hot snacks which are sure to please. Serve them to the family and friends after a day's outing; at lunchtime, tea or suppertime; serve with mugs of coffee or cocoa topped with whipped cream.

Triple Deckers

> *Preparation time: 5 minutes*
> *Cooking time: 10-15 minutes*
> *Special remarks: peeled, chopped, tomatoes could be used instead of mushrooms*
> *For 4-6 servings*

> 2 hardboiled eggs, chopped
> 6 ounces cooked ham, chopped or minced
> 1 teaspoon made mustard
> 4 ounces mushrooms, fried and chopped
> salt and pepper
> 12 slices white bread
> butter for spreading

Mix the hardboiled eggs, ham, mustard, mushrooms and seasoning. Spread one side of each slice of bread with butter. Divide half the ham mixture between 4 slices of bread and cover with another slice of bread. Cover with remaining ham mixture. Top with remaining bread slices, buttered side down. Brush the top of the sandwiches with a little melted butter. Place on a baking sheet. Bake at 375°F, or Gas Mark 5, until crisp.

Toasted Sweet Sandwiches

Mix 4 ounces cottage cheese with 1 egg and 1 tablespoon sugar. Spread 4 slices bread with the mixture. Top each with another slice. Dip each sandwich in 2 eggs beaten with 6 tablespoons milk. Brown on both sides in hot butter in a frying pan or electric skillet. Serve with jam.

A toasted sandwich and a mug of hot soup make a delicious snack meal. Try tomato soup and toasted sandwiches filled with flaked canned salmon, mixed with chopped, hardboiled eggs, and bound with a little mayonnaise.

Crispy Rolls

Preparation time: 5 minutes
Cooking time: 15-20 minutes
Special remarks: these rolls are popular for teenage parties

crisp rolls as required
butter or margarine, for spreading
made mustard
1 slice bologna ⎫
1 slice cooked ham ⎬ per roll
2 slices salami ⎪
2 triangles cheese ⎭
pieces of aluminium foil

Split rolls and spread both sides with butter or margarine. Spread with mustard and arrange filling on each roll. Add tops of rolls. Wrap tightly in foil and place on a baking sheet. Bake in a very hot oven, 450°F, or Gas Mark 8, for about 20 minutes.

T.V. Supper Special

Preparation time: 5 minutes
Cooking time: 5 minutes
Special remarks: the sandwiches may be grilled or cooked in the electric frying pan
For each person you require

1 tablespoon baked beans
1 rasher bacon, roughly chopped
2 slices brown bread
1 slice cheese
a little mustard
butter or bacon fat, melted

Heat the baked beans and grill or fry the bacon. Butter one slice of bread and add beans and cooked bacon. Cover with a slice of cheese. Spread remaining slice of bread with prepared mustard. Press lightly mustard side down onto filling. Brush top with melted bacon fat or butter. Arrange on electric frying pan or grill pan. Cook until brown and toasted, turning once.

Decorate with sliced gherkins and pineapple rings.

Try a quick soup like Quick Farmhouse Chowder (see page 8) and a selection of sandwiches. Weight-watchers choose starch-reduced bread or rolls and a cottage cheese and chopped apple filling.

Corned Beef Toasty

Spread toasted bread or rusk bread slices generously with butter. Add a layer of prepared coleslaw salad and 2 slices corned beef. Top with a skewered baby tomato and spring onion.

Vienna Rolls

Split rolls lengthwise but do not cut all the way through at the back, so that a lid is formed. Spread with butter or margarine. Cover roll with crisp lettuce, cheese strips, and folded slices of ham, luncheon meat, chopped ham, or pork roll. Top with hardboiled egg slices and moisten with a little French dressing or mayonnaise.

Tuna Rolls

For six people, mix 1 (6½-7-ounce) can tuna with 1 tablespoon lemon juice. Add 2 chopped, hard-boiled eggs, 2 tablespoons chopped spring onions, salt and pepper.

Toast or leave plain 6 soft rolls or baps. Spread thickly with butter and add a few lettuce leaves and tomato slices. Divide tuna filling between each roll. Garnish with a little mayonnaise or salad cream.

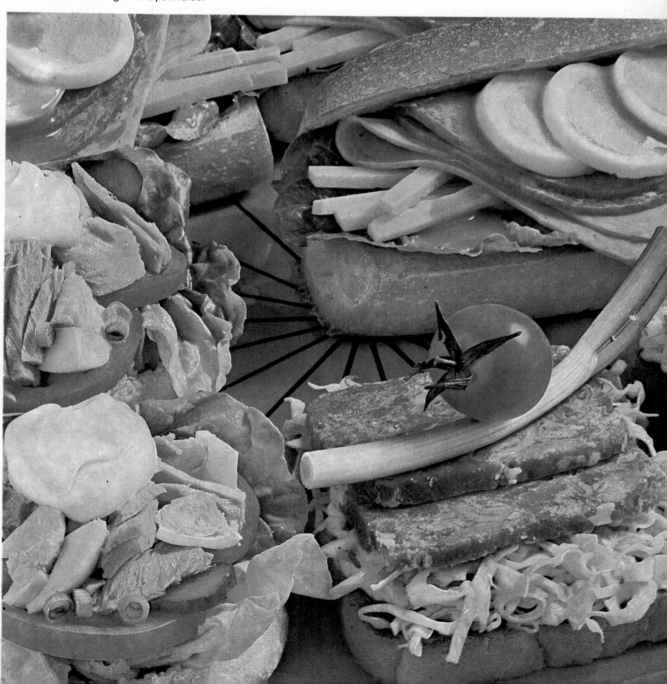

CHAPTER 10

Quick Baking

Everyone loves the flavour of home-baked cakes and biscuits. Many of them can be made very simply and quickly using easy-mix recipes and quick-creaming fats.

Surprise Cookies

Preparation time: 10 minutes
Cooking time: 10-15 minutes
Special remarks: for best results you must use plain (dark) chocolate. Use 2 teaspoons to put the mixture on the baking sheet (see illustration)
For about 12 cookies

4 ounces luxury margarine
2 ounces caster sugar
few drops vanilla essence
5 ounces plain flour
pinch salt
2 ounces plain chocolate

Cream fat and sugar until white and fluffy and add the vanilla essence. Stir in the flour, sieved with the salt. The mixture should be fairly stiff. Heat a large chopping knife or dip in boiling water. Chop the chocolate into small pieces (heating the knife makes this easier). Mix chocolate into biscuit mixture. Place teaspoons of mixture on a greased baking sheet. Bake in a fairly hot oven, 375°F, or Gas Mark 5, until pale golden brown. Cool on a wire tray.

Susan's Malt Loaf

Preparation time: 5 minutes plus overnight maturing time
Cooking time: 1¼ hours
Special remarks: use the same cup to measure all ingredients
For one loaf

1 cup bran breakfast cereal
1 cup soft brown sugar
1 cup sultanas
1 cup milk
1 cup self-raising flour

Mix all ingredients together in a bowl, except the flour. Leave overnight. Next day, stir in the flour and pour into a greased loaf tin. Bake in a moderate oven, 350°F, or Gas Mark 4.

Quick Milk Rolls

Preparation time: 10 minutes
Cooking time: 15-20 minutes
Special remarks: these quick rolls are ideal if you have run out of bread, or they can be served as Devonshire splits, cut open and filled with cream and jam. The rolls should be eaten the day they are made as they don't keep well

8 ounces plain flour
¼ teaspoon salt
2 level teaspoons baking powder
1 ounce butter or margarine
1 egg, beaten
scant ¼ pint milk

Sieve flour, salt and baking powder into a basin. Rub in butter or margarine as lightly as possible. Make a well in centre and add the egg and enough milk to make a soft dough. Mix quickly and lightly, then turn on to a floured board and form into small balls. Put on a greased and floured baking sheet. Bake at once in a very hot oven, 450°F or Gas Mark 8. When ready brush with a little milk or melted butter to glaze them. Do not open door for first 15 minutes.

Grease and line each sandwich tin with a circle of greaseproof paper.

Sieve flour and baking powder into a large baking bowl. Add remaining ingredients and mix well. Beat for 2 minutes. Divide evenly between the 2 tins. Bake in the centre of a warm oven, 325°F or Gas Mark 3, until risen and firm to the touch. Cool and sandwich together with jam and butter cream.

Unbaked Butterscotch Cookies

Preparation time: 10 minutes
Cooking time: nil
Special remarks: leave cookies to set for at least 2 hours
For 2½ dozen cookies

8 ounces granulated sugar
6 ounces butter or margarine
1 (3-ounce) can evaporated milk
½ a 4-ounce packet instant butterscotch or caramel whip
5 ounces rolled oats

In a large saucepan mix the sugar, butter or margarine and evaporated milk. Heat to a full rolling boil, stirring frequently. Remove from heat and add the instant whip and oats. Beat thoroughly together. Cool for 15 minutes. Drop teaspoonfuls on a greaseproof paper lined tray. Leave to set.

One-Stage Sandwich Cake

Preparation time: 5 minutes
Cooking time: 25-35 minutes
Special remarks: It is essential to the success of this cake that you use a luxury margarine, e.g. Superfine or Blue Band
For 2 (7-inch) sandwich tins

4 ounces self-raising flour
1 level teaspoon baking powder
4 ounces luxury margarine, cut in pieces
4 ounces caster sugar
2 eggs
jam and butter cream, for filling

Orange and Nut Biscuits

Preparation time: 15 minutes
Cooking time: 20-25 minutes
Special remarks: the biscuit mixture may be refrigerated before baking, if preferred
For about 2 dozen biscuits

8 ounces plain flour
pinch salt
3 ounces butter or margarine
4 ounces caster sugar
grated rind of ½ orange
1 egg, separated
3-4 tablespoons orange juice
4 ounces almonds or walnuts, roughly chopped

Sift flour and salt. Rub in the butter or margarine. Stir in the sugar, orange rind, nuts, egg yolk and orange juice to give a fairly firm dough. Roll into small balls and flatten slightly. Brush with lightly whisked egg white and place on greased baking sheets. Bake in a moderate oven, 350°F or Gas Mark 4, until lightly browned. Dust with sugar while hot.

SECTION THREE
Hospitality in a Hurry

CHAPTER 11
Dinner Parties

In this section you will find ideas for entertaining small groups of people to dinner parties as well as larger numbers to informal supper parties.

Giving a dinner party for a small number of people is one of the nicest ways of entertaining friends. However, if it is to be fun for you as well as the guests, it must·be carefully planned. Two or three courses followed by cheese and coffee is the usual number so try to choose one really exciting dish and let the others be cold or something which can be prepared in advance.

PARTY MENU 1
Melon Slices with Ginger
and Sugar
Veal scallopini
Buttered Noodles
Tossed Green Salad
Ice Cream and Chocolate Sauce

Veal Scallopini

Preparation time: 20 minutes
Cooking time: 30-40 minutes
Special remarks: ¼ pint white wine may be added instead of stock, if preferred
For 4 servings

4 rashers bacon, rind removed and diced
2 medium onions, chopped
1 clove garlic, crushed
1 tablespoon each oil and butter
1 pound leg or fillet of veal
¼-½ pint stock
1 teaspoon paprika pepper
½ teaspoon sugar
1 tablespoon tomato paste
1 (16-ounce) can tomatoes
8 ounces mushrooms, sliced
8 ounces noodles

Fry bacon until crisp and remove from pan. Fry onions and garlic over moderate heat until soft and golden brown—about 5 minutes. Remove from pan. Add oil and butter.

Cut meat into pieces and beat slightly to flatten. Dip·in seasoned flour. Brown meat, a little at a time. Return bacon and onions to pan with meat. Stir in stock, paprika, salt, sugar, tomato paste, canned tomatoes, juice and mushrooms. Bring to the boil, stirring all the time. Reduce heat and cover. Simmer until tender adding more stock if necessary. Sprinkle with parsley.

Meanwhile add the noodles to a pan of boiling, salted water. Heat to boiling point and cook for 10 minutes. Drain and return noodles to pan with butter. Toss and serve around the meat.

PARTY MENU 2
Baked Pork Chops and Pineapple
Savoury Rice
Buttered Broccoli
Strawberry Cooler

Baked Pork Chops and Pineapple

Preparation time: 20 minutes
Cooking time: 50 minutes
Special remarks: this is a very easily pre-
pared meal with no last-minute pre-
paration. Use frozen broccoli and cook
as directed on packet. Drain and add a
few drops lemon juice, seasoning and
butter
For 6 servings

6 thick pork chops
salt and pepper
1 (10-ounce) can pineapple rings
6 tablespoons brown sugar
1 teaspoon ground ginger
SAVOURY RICE:
12 ounces long grain rice
1 small onion, finely chopped
2 ounces butter
scant 1¼ pints (24 fluid ounces) chicken
stock
salt and pepper

Trim chops and arrange in an ovenproof dish; season. Add enough pineapple juice to come half-way up the chops. Cover closely with foil and the lid. Bake in a moderate oven, 350°F or Gas Mark 4, until tender.

Meanwhile prepare savoury rice. Melt butter in a shallow casserole, add onion, cover and cook over low heat for 10 minutes. Add rice and stir until grains are coated with butter. Stir in chicken stock and seasoning. Cover and bake below the pork chops for about 40 minutes or until rice is tender.

Just before serving garnish each chop with a pineapple ring and sprinkle with brown sugar and ginger. Return to the oven, uncovered, for about 10 minutes, until glazed.

Strawberry Cooler

Preparation time: 10 minutes plus setting
time
Cooking time: nil

Special remarks: frozen strawberries may
be used—allow to defrost completely
and use the juice to take the place of
some of the water
For 6 servings

1 (16-ounce) can cherries
½ orange jelly
¼ pint water, boiling
1 pound fresh strawberries
1 teaspoon lemon juice
¼ pint thick fresh cream

Dissolve orange jelly in ¼ pint boiling water. Measure juice from cherries, add cold water if necessary to make ¼ pint. Add to jelly with lemon juice. Leave to cool until syrupy. Add sliced strawberries and stoned cherries. Divide fruit and jelly between 6 glasses. Leave to set and decorate with whipped, sweetened fresh cream.

PARTY MENU 3

Sherried Consommé and
Melba Toast
Kebabs with Barbecue Sauce
Boiled Rice
American Frosted Cream

Sherried Consommé

Preparation time: 5 minutes
Cooking time: 5-10 minutes plus time for
  toast
Special remarks: canned clear soups are
  made extra special with the addition of
  a little sherry
For 4 servings

2 cans consommé
water to dilute, as directed
6 tablespoons dry sherry
4-8 slices stale bread, cut very thinly

Make melba toast: lay the slices of bread on baking sheets and dry off in the bottom of a very cool oven until they are crisp and curled. Just before serving brown slightly under a very low grill.

Dilute consommé as directed on can. Add the sherry and heat slowly. Serve very hot with melba toast.

Kebabs with Barbecue Sauce

Preparation time: overnight marinading
  time and 20 minutes
Cooking time: about 20-30 minutes
Special remarks: marinading the meat
  overnight makes it tender and full of
  flavour
For 4 servings

1¼ pounds tender lean beef or lamb
1 large onion, sliced
salt and freshly ground black pepper

2 tablespoons lemon juice
4 tablespoons oil
1 bay leaf
8 small tomatoes
6 ounces mushrooms, cleaned
1 green pepper, de-seeded and sliced
8 ounces button onions, parboiled
BARBECUE SAUCE:
2 ounces butter
1 teaspoon tomato paste
2 tablespoons vinegar
2 tablespoons brown sugar
2 teaspoons dry mustard
1 tablespoon Worcester sauce
¼ pint water

Cut meat in cubes discarding gristle and fat. Put in a glass or china bowl and add the sliced onion, seasoning, lemon juice, oil and bay leaf. Mix well. Cover and leave to marinate overnight, stirring once or twice.

Next day make barbecue sauce: melt butter and fry the drained onion used in the marinade until soft. Stir in remaining sauce ingredients. Simmer for 5 minutes.

About 30 minutes before serving thread the meat on skewers with the tomatoes, mushrooms, green pepper and button onions. Arrange in the bottom of the grill pan. Pour barbecue sauce over and grill under moderate heat. Turn skewers over and baste frequently with sauce.

Serve on a bed of fluffy boiled rice.

American Frosted Cream

Preparation time: 10 minutes
Freezing time: 3-4 hours altogether
Special remarks: this delicately flavoured
  sweet is very refreshing after kebabs
For 4 servings

4 ounces cheese
3 ounces caster sugar
1 teaspoon vanilla essence
½ pint thin cream
strawberries or raspberries, to decorate
petit four biscuits, to serve

Beat the cream cheese until soft, beat in the sugar and vanilla essence. Slowly add the cream mixing well between each addition. Freeze in the ice tray of the refrigerator until partially frozen. Spoon into a bowl and whisk until smooth. Pour back into tray and freeze until firm. Decorate with sliced fruit.

```
●●●●●●●●●●●●●●●●●●●●●●●●●●●●●●●
```

PARTY MENU 4
Cream of Mushroom Soup
and Croûtons
Poached Salmon Steaks
New Potatoes
Buttered Asparagus
Super Peach Flan

```
●●●●●●●●●●●●●●●●●●●●●●●●●●●●●●●
```

Cream of Mushroom Soup

Preparation time: 10 minutes
Cooking time: about 30 minutes
Special remarks: do not reheat the soup after adding the cream and egg yolk or it may curdle
For 4 servings

8 ounces mushrooms, cleaned and sliced
1 medium onion, finely chopped
½ pint stock
1 ounce butter
1 level tablespoon flour
¾ pint milk
salt and freshly ground black pepper
little grated nutmeg
2-3 thin slices white bread
butter or oil for frying
1 egg yolk
2-3 tablespoons cream

Put the mushrooms, onion and stock in a pan. Cover and simmer for 20 minutes. Rub through a sieve or purée in the liquidiser.

In a saucepan melt the butter and stir in the flour. Gradually stir in the milk, beating well between each addition. Add the mushroom and onion purée and season to taste with salt, pepper and nutmeg. Simmer gently for 10 minutes.

Meanwhile dice the bread and fry until golden brown in hot fat. Remove pan from heat. Drain well. Blend egg yolk and cream together and mix with 2-3 tablespoons of the hot soup. Stir into remaining soup and serve.

Poached Salmon Steaks

Preparation time: 5 minutes
Cooking time: about 10 minutes depending on thickness
Special remarks: fish is attractive and quickly cooked for dinner parties when time is short

For 4 servings
4 salmon steaks or cutlets
2-3 ounces butter, melted
parsley sprigs and lemon wedges
COURT BOUILLON:
½ pint water or dry white wine
rind and juice of ½ lemon
1 bay leaf
2 peppercorns
1 sprig parsley
½ teaspoon salt
1 small onion, sliced

Wipe the fish and arrange the pieces in one layer in a large shallow casserole or frying pan. Add the ingredients for court bouillon. Cover with foil and the lid. Bring slowly to the boil. Draw pan from heat, remove lid and leave in cooking liquid for about a minute. Drain carefully and arrange in serving dish. Pour melted butter over.

Super Peach Flan

Preparation time: 10 minutes
Cooking time: 7 minutes
Special remarks: place the bowl of hot glaze in a pan of cold water—it will cool and start to set much more quickly
For 4 servings

1 baked sponge flan case
1 (15-ounce) can halved peaches
2 tablespoons sugar
2 heaped tablespoons apricot jam
squeeze lemon juice
shredded almonds
thick whipped cream, for decoration
2 ounces chocolate, grated

Put the flan case on a serving dish. Drain juice from peaches and measure 2 tablespoons of the juice into a small saucepan. Add sugar, jam and lemon juice. Heat slowly and when jam has melted boil rapidly without a lid for about 5 minutes. Rub through a sieve and leave to cool until mixture begins to thicken slightly.

Meanwhile arrange fruit in flan case and toast the almonds for a few minutes under a low grill.

Carefully pour glaze over fruit and sprinkle with half the almonds. Spread the whipped cream over and scatter with remaining almonds and chocolate.

PARTY MENU 5
Florida Cocktail
Steak Diane
Baked Potatoes
Braised Celery
Fudge Sundae

Florida Cocktail

Preparation time: 10 minutes
Cooking time: nil
Special remarks: alternatively use canned
*   orange and grapefruit segments*
For 4 servings

2 grapefruit, cut in segments
2 oranges, cut in segments
sugar to taste
4 maraschino cherries

Mix the prepared segments and divide between serving glasses. Pour over any juice collected while preparing fruit. Sprinkle with sugar and decorate with a cherry. Chill if possible.

Steak Diane

Preparation time: 5 minutes
Cooking time: about 5 minutes altogether
Special remarks: fried or grilled steaks
*   should be served freshly cooked*
For 4 servings

6-8 ounces mushrooms
2 tablespoons oil
2 ounces butter
4 fillet steaks, ½ inch thick
salt and freshly ground black pepper
1 teaspoon dry mustard
2 tablespoons lemon juice
2 teaspoons freshly chopped chives
1 tablespoon Worcester sauce

Flute the mushroom caps and fry in half the butter and oil for about 5 minutes. Meanwhile sprinkle one side of each steak with salt, pepper and a pinch of the mustard. Pound into the meat with a meat mallet. Turn meat over and pound other side until meat is about ⅓ inch in thickness.

Melt remaining butter and oil in separate frying pan. When sizzling hot, add meat and cook for 2 minutes on each side. Transfer meat to a hot serving dish and add the fried mushrooms, lemon juice, chives and Worcester sauce to the pan. Bring to the boil, stirring well. Pour sauce over meat and serve at once.

BAKED POTATOES: prepare 4 large potatoes as indicated on page 42. When cooked remove insides and mix with 2 tablespoons fresh cream, season and put back into potato jackets. Sprinkle with fried, crumbled bacon. Serve hot.

Fudge Sundae

Preparation time: 5 minutes
Cooking time: 5 minutes
Special remarks: chocolate should be
*   heated slowly or it is inclined to*
*   separate*
For 4 servings

6 ounces plain (dark) chocolate
1 (4-ounce) can evaporated milk
2 teaspoons instant coffee powder
1 (small) block vanilla ice cream
1 (small) block chocolate ice cream
a few chopped walnuts
wafer biscuits, to serve

Put chocolate and evaporated milk in a bowl over a pan of hot water. Heat gently until chocolate melts and mixture blends. Dissolve coffee powder in 1 tablespoon boiling water and add to sauce. Stir well and cool for a few minutes. Pour a little sauce into each serving dish and add spoonfuls of ice cream alternating with chocolate and vanilla. Pour more sauce over the top and sprinkle with walnuts.

CHAPTER 12

Informal Parties

Easy Salads

This type of party is ideal for larger numbers of people. The idea is to have lots of tempting salads served with a selection of cold meats or a hot dish such as pizza, risotto, savoury flans or oven-fried chicken. You might like to serve hot soup first or perhaps gâteaux, meringues or fruit flans for dessert. If time is very short serve fresh fruit or a good selection of cheeses.

Salads can be prepared in advance but keep them covered until you are ready to serve. Green salads should be mixed with a very little French dressing, if mixed with too much they tend to go limp quickly.

Coleslaw salad (see page 45) is popular for parties. Serve in a large bowl garnished with radish roses

Sweet Corn and Rice Salad

Preparation time: 5 minutes
Cooking time: 15 minutes for rice
Special remarks: this salad can be pre-
pared in advance

For 8 servings
  salad cream or mayonnaise
  1 teaspoon dry mustard
  1 pound long grain rice, cooked and
    rinsed with cold water
  1 (large) can pineapple, drained and
    chopped
  4 sticks celery, scrubbed and chopped
  1 (large) can sweet corn

Blend about 6 tablespoons mayonnaise or salad cream with 2-3 tablespoons liquid from the can of sweet corn. Stir in the mustard. Add remaining ingredients and mix well. The salad should be fairly moist—add more salad cream or mayonnaise if necessary.

Special Baked Chicken

Preparation time: 10 minutes
Cooking time: 45-60 minutes
Special remarks: buy a chicken and joint
it yourself or buy loose chicken joints
For 8 servings

  8 chicken joints
  seasoned flour
  1 egg, beaten
  dry breadcrumbs
  2 tablespoons sesame seed, optional
  2-3 ounces bacon fat or butter

Coat chicken joints with seasoned flour. Dip first in egg then breadcrumbs mixed with sesame seed. Melt bacon fat or butter in a roasting tin. Add the joints and bake in a hot oven, 400°F or Gas Mark 6, until tender. Baste joints occasionally and turn once.

Serve hot garnished with parsley.

Cheese-Bacon Potatoes

Preparation time: 10 minutes
Cooking time: 1¼ hours
Special remarks: baked potatoes are wonderful for parties—they are easy to prepare and can be stuffed with a variety of fillings
For 8-10 servings

8 medium potatoes, scrubbed
1 (5-ounce) carton sour cream
2 ounces cheese
scant ¼ pint milk
2 ounces butter or margarine
salt and pepper
4-6 rashers bacon, fried and crumbled

Brush potatoes with oil or rub with lard—this keeps the skins soft. Bake in a hot oven, 400°F or Gas Mark 6, until cooked—about 1 hour.

Cut a lengthwise slice from top of each potato and scoop out the centre, taking care to keep skins intact. Mash potato and add sour cream, cheese, milk, butter and seasoning. Beat until fluffy preferably with electric mixer. Spoon mixture back into skins. Place on a baking sheet and return to hot oven for a further 15 minutes until piping hot. Sprinkle bacon over.

Potato Salad

Preparation time: 10 minutes
Cooking time: 30-40 minutes
Special remarks: potato salad made this way has a delicious flavour
For 8-10 servings

2 pounds potatoes, scrubbed
about 4 tablespoons mayonnaise or salad cream
about 3 tablespoons milk
salt and freshly ground black pepper
¼ teaspoon grated nutmeg
2 tablespoons freshly chopped parsley
1 bunch spring onion tops or chives, chopped
1 teaspoon dry mustard

Put whole unpeeled potatoes in a pan of boiling salted water. Cook until tender, 30-40 minutes, depending on size.

Meanwhile in a salad bowl blend the mayonnaise or salad cream, milk, seasoning, nutmeg, parsley and chopped spring onion tops or chives until well mixed.

When potatoes are just cooked, drain and peel. Chop roughly and mix carefully while hot with the dressing mixture.

Salami Salad

Preparation time: 10 minutes
Cooking time: nil
Special remarks: use half the amount of dressing if salad is to be prepared a long time in advance—serve rest separately
For 8 servings

DRESSING:
1 tablespoon lemon juice
1 tablespoon vinegar
¼ teaspoon dry mustard
salt and freshly ground black pepper
4 tablespoons salad oil
SALAD:
2 lettuces, washed
4 tomatoes, cut in wedges
2-3 sticks celery, sliced
1 onion, finely sliced
1 bunch watercress, washed
4 ounces salami, thinly sliced

Put all dressing ingredients in a screwtop bottle—shake vigorously.

Tear lettuce in pieces and put all ingredients in salad bowl. Pour dressing over and toss.

HOT BUFFET FOR 6 GUESTS

This is the ideal way to entertain when you don't
want all the work of a full-scale dinner party

Grilled Steak Sandwich

Preparation time: 15 minutes
Cooking time: about 4-6 minutes
*Special remarks: this buffet party is
especially popular with men and teen-
agers*

1 pound frying steak, cut ¼ inch thick
steak seasoning
2 ounces butter
3 tablespoons oil
2 onions, chopped
1 rounded tablespoon flour
½ pint stock, hot
salt and pepper
2 tablespoons bottled steak sauce
1 tablespoon Worcester sauce
12 slices French bread

Heat 2 tablespoons oil in a small thick saucepan.
Add chopped onions and fry until lightly browned.
Stir in the flour and cook for a few minutes.
Gradually add the hot stock. Bring to the boil,
stirring constantly until thickened. Stir in seasoning, steak sauce and Worcester sauce. Keep hot.
   Cut steak in 6 pieces. Season with steak
seasoning and beat with a meat mallet. Heat
butter and remaining oil in a large frying pan or
brush steaks with oil and grill. Cook steaks for 2-3
minutes each side.
   Toast bread. To serve, dip toast quickly in
sauce; top with steak and remaining toast also
dipped in sauce. Serve hot.

Herbed tomato slices

see page 45

Coleslaw or Green Salad

see page 44

Coffee and Rum Creams

*Preparation time: 10 minutes not in-
cluding chilling time*
Cooking time: 5 minutes
*Special remarks: vary the flavour by
omitting rum and adding 1 teaspoon
vanilla essence*

1½ ounces cornflour
1 pint milk
2 ounces caster sugar
1 ounce butter
3 tablespoons bottled coffee essence
**3 tablespoons rum or 1 teaspoon rum
essence**
3 eggs, separated
1 small carton thick cream

Put cornflour in a small saucepan. Blend in the
milk. Heat, stirring constantly until mixture boils
and thickens—cook for 2 minutes. Remove from
heat and stir in half the sugar, butter, coffee essence
and rum. Beat in each egg yolk. Whisk egg whites
until stiff and firm. Whisk in remaining sugar
quickly—do not over whisk. Fold whites into hot
custard mixture. Pour into individual glass dishes
and chill. Decorate with whipped cream just before
serving.

HOT BUFFET FOR 8 GUESTS

Chicken Bake

Preparation time: 10 minutes
Cooking time: about 30 minutes altogether
Special remarks: alternatively omit some of the chicken and add an equal quantity of chopped cooked ham

1 pound ribbon noodles
1 ounce butter or margarine
1 can condensed chicken soup
1 soup can milk
salt and pepper
1-1½ pounds cooked chicken, diced
1 (small) can pimiento, chopped
4 ounces dried breadcrumbs, crushed
1 ounce butter or margarine, melted
4 ounces Cheddar cheese, grated

Cook noodles in boiling, salted water for 10 minutes. Drain and rinse with boiling water. Put back in pan and add butter or margarine, soup, milk, diced chicken and chopped pimiento. Heat gently and pour into a buttered serving dish.

Mix breadcrumbs with melted butter or margarine. Sprinkle around edge of chicken dish. Cover with grated cheese. Bake in a moderate oven, 350°F or Gas Mark 4, for 15-20 minutes.

Mixed Vegetables

Preparation time: 5 minutes
Cooking time: 10-15 minutes

Special remarks: canned vegetables may be used instead of frozen

4 ounces frozen peas
4 ounces frozen broad beans
4 ounces frozen cut green beans
4 ounces frozen sweet corn
2 ounces butter
1 onion, chopped
2 teaspoons sugar
salt and pepper
1 tablespoon parsley, chopped

Cook frozen vegetables according to packet directions. Drain.

Meanwhile cook the chopped onion in hot butter until soft but not browned. Stir in the sugar, seasoning, parsley and cooked vegetables. Serve in a hot vegetable dish.

Hot Herb Bread

Cream together 4 ounces butter, 1 tablespoon lemon juice, 1 tablespoon chopped parsley and 1 teaspoon dried herbs. Slit a French loaf diagonally into slices, leaving bottom crust whole. Spread both sides of each slice with flavoured butter. Wrap in foil and place in a hot oven, 400°F or Gas Mark 6, for 20 minutes or until hot. Serve from the foil.

Quick Bites and Snacks

Cheese Pastry Bites

Preparation time: 15 minutes
Cooking time: 10-12 minutes
Special remarks: if you have time allow
pastry to rest or chill for 1 hour before
baking
For 3 dozen bites

6 ounces plain flour
salt and pepper
pinch cayenne pepper
good pinch dry mustard
3 ounces Cheddar cheese, grated
2 egg yolks
little cold water
15 small stuffed green olives

Sieve flour with salt, pepper, cayenne and mustard. Rub in margarine until mixture resembles fine breadcrumbs, as for shortcrust pastry. Mix in the cheese. Add the egg yolks and a little water, stirring until ingredients begin to stick together. Collect dough together, knead very lightly and quickly. Divide dough in half. Using one half roll out dough to $\frac{1}{8}$ inch in thickness. Cut into suitable sized rounds and wrap around each olive. Roll out other half of dough into a $\frac{1}{4}$-inch thick rectangle. With a pastry wheel or knife cut into sticks $\frac{1}{2}$ inch wide and 4 inches long. Place olive balls and sticks on ungreased baking sheets. Bake in a hot oven, 425°F or Gas Mark 7, until golden brown.

Stuffed Sausages or Frankfurters

Slit frankfurters lengthwise but not all way through. Stuff with strips of pickled gherkin and cheese. Wrap half a bacon rasher round each sausage or frankfurter and secure with toothpicks. Grill for 5-7 minutes turning once. Or bake in a fairly hot oven, 375°F or Gas Mark 5, for 15 minutes.

Other fillings include: canned ham pâté; mustard and strips of pineapple or mashed potatoes flavoured with cheese.

This dish is ideal for unexpected guests as you can use canned frankfurters.

Curry Puffs

Preparation time: 10 minutes
Cooking time: 10-15 minutes
Special remarks: use packet savoury sauce
and flavour with curry powder to taste.
Heat together
For 8-10 puffs

4 ounces frozen puff pastry, thawed
4-ounce packet frozen shrimps, thawed
$\frac{1}{4}$ pint thick curry-flavoured white sauce
1 egg, beaten

Roll out pastry thinly and cut into rounds, using a $1\frac{1}{2}$-inch plain cutter. Mix curry sauce and shrimps and put a teaspoon of the mixture into centres of half the pastry rounds. Brush edges with water and put the other pastry rounds on top. Press edges together and flute them. Brush with egg and bake in a very hot oven, 450°F or Gas Mark 8, until well risen and golden brown.

BASIC METHODS OF COOKING

BAKING—cooking in dry heat in the oven.

BOILING—cooking food in a boiling liquid (212°F), eg. vegetables, pasta and boiled puddings.

BRAISING—meat is browned then cooked slowly on a bed of vegetables with very little liquid, in a covered container.

FRYING—Shallow frying is cooking in just enough fat to cover the base of the pan. It is a quick method of cooking.
Deep frying is cooking food by immersing in a deep pan filled two-thirds full of hot fat or oil.

GRILLING—always pre-heat the grill for this method of cooking and brush the grill rack with fat. Food which is to be completely cooked by grilling should be cooked at a high temperature for the initial browning period. Then reduce the heat and complete the cooking.

POACHING—cooking food gently in liquid at simmering temperature (185-200°F).

POT ROASTING—a combination of frying and steaming. The meat is browned and then cooked in a heavy covered casserole or saucepan with fat only. It is a slow method of roasting and may be carried out on top of the stove or in the oven at a low temperature.

PRESSURE COOKING—cooking food at a very high temperature under pressure. The food cooks quickly and tougher types of meat are made more tender. Types of pressure cookers vary and the makers instructions should be followed explicitly.

ROASTING—cooking food at a high temperature in the oven. The container is open and little fat should be used.

SAUTÉ—To cook over a strong heat in a small amount of fat or oil, shaking the pan frequently to prevent sticking.

SIMMERING—cooking below boiling point—the liquid should bubble gently at the side of the pot.

STEAMING—using the steam from boiling water to cook food. The food may be cooked in a steamer over boiling water or the basin of food may be stood in the boiling water. Always cover the saucepan or steamer.

STEWING—cooking food at simmering point or below in a liquid. It is a long slow method of cooking and an excellent way of tenderising the tougher cuts of meat. Stewing is carried out in a covered container.

COOKING TERMS

BAIN MARIE—a roasting tin half filled with water in which a dish of food which must be baked slowly is placed before cooking in the oven, e.g. caramel custards.

BAKING BLIND—the method of baking flans, tarts and other pastry cases without a filling. Put the flan ring or pie dish on a baking sheet and line with pastry. Cut a circle of greaseproof paper slightly larger than the flan. Fill with dried beans, rice, or bread crusts to weigh the paper down. Bake the flan for 15 minutes. Remove the greaseproof paper and beans and bake a further 10 minutes to brown and crisp the pastry. Cool.

BASTING—spooning the cooking fat and liquid over food while roasting. This keeps the food moist, adds flavour and improves the appearance.

BEATING—method of introducing air to a mixture, a wooden spoon, wire whisk or electric beater may be used for this process.

BINDING—adding a liquid, egg or melted fat to a dry mixture to hold it together, e.g. beaten egg is added to mince for hamburgers.

BLANCHING—putting food in boiling water in order to either whiten, remove the skin, salt or strong flavour from food.

BLENDING—the process of mixing a thickening agent, such as flour or cornflour with a little cold water to a smooth paste. A little of the hot liquid to be thickened is then added to the paste and the whole returned to the saucepan. The mixture is stirred until it boils and thickens. Used to thicken the liquid of casseroles, stews and certain sauces.

BOUQUET GARNI—a bunch of fresh mixed herbs tied together with string and used for flavouring. Usually a bay leaf, sprig of parsley, sprig of thyme and perhaps a few celery leaves. Dried herbs may be used tied in a little muslin bag.

BROWNING—putting a cooked dish or meringue under the grill, or in the oven for a short time to give it an appetising golden colour.

CASSEROLE—baking dish usually ovenproof earthenware, pottery, porcelain or cast-iron with a tight fitting lid. Food cooked in a casserole is served straight from the dish.

CHINING—method of preparing neck or loin joints for easier carving. The bone at the wide end of the chops or cutlets is cut away from the meat so that it may be carved into portions of each rib each.

CHOPPING—dividing food into very small pieces on a chopping board using a very sharp knife.

COATING—covering food with a thin layer of flour, egg, breadcrumbs or batter before it is fried.

CONSISTENCY—term describing the texture (usually the thickness) of a mixture.

CREAMING—beating together fat and sugar to incorporate air, break down the sugar crystals and soften the fat.

FOLDING IN—to incorporate two mixtures using a light over and over motion. Usually applied to light mixtures such as whisked egg white or cream which have to be folded into other ingredients. It is important to carry out the process carefully so that the air is not knocked out of the light mixture. Flour is sifted over whisked egg mixtures for very light sponge cakes. The use of an electric mixer is not practical for this process. A sharp edged metal spoon is ideal for folding in.

GLAZE—a liquid brushed over the surface of a dish to give it a shiny finish.

GRATE—shaving food into shreds.

HULL—remove stalks from soft fruits—strawberries, raspberries etc.

KNEADING—working a dough using the fingertips for pastry-making and the knuckles for bread-making. The edges of the dough are drawn to the centre.

MARINADE—a liquid made of oil and wine, vinegar or lemon juice and flavouring vegetables, herbs and spices. Food is steeped in the marinade to tenderise and add flavour.

PURÉE—fresh or cooked fruit or vegetables are broken down into a smooth pulp by sieving, pounding or blending in the liquidiser.

REDUCING—boiling a liquid, uncovered, in order to evaporate the water content and make the liquid more concentrated.

ROUX—a thickening agent for soups and sauces. Equal quantities of fat and flour are cooked together.

RUBBING IN—a method of incorporating fat into flour, e.g. in short-crust pastry making. Add the fat in small pieces to the flour. Using the fingertips, quickly and lightly rub the fat into the flour, lifting the hands as you do this.

SEASONED FLOUR—mix 1 teaspoon of salt, a good sprinkling of pepper and 2 tablespoons flour. Use to coat food before cooking.

SIEVING—to rub food through a sieve using a wooden spoon, in order to discard skin, stalks or seeds.

SKIMMING—to remove the scum or fat from food whilst it is cooking. A piece of absorbent kitchen paper or a metal spoon are used.

STOCK—a well-flavoured liquid made by simmering meat and/or vegetables in water for a prolonged period, to extract the flavour. When time is short the commercial stock cubes may be substituted.

SWEATING—cooking foods, usually vegetables in a small amount of fat to soften and add flavour. The pan is always covered.

WATER BATH—see Bain marie.

WHIPPING OR WHISKING—adding air quickly to a mixture by beating with a hand whisk, rotary beater or electric beater.

ZEST—the thin coloured skin of citrus fruit which contains the oil and flavour.